Routledge Revivals

Mercantilism and the East India Trade

Mercantilism
and the
East India Trade

P.J.Thomas

Routledge
Taylor & Francis Group

First published in 1926 by Frank Cass & Co. Ltd

This edition first published in 2019 by Routledge
2 Park Square, Milton Park, Abingdon, Oxon, OX14 4RN
and by Routledge
52 Vanderbilt Avenue, New York, NY 10017, USA

Routledge is an imprint of the Taylor & Francis Group, an informa business

© 1926 by Taylor & Francis

Publisher's Note
The publisher has gone to great lengths to ensure the quality of this reprint but points out that some imperfections in the original copies may be apparent.

Disclaimer
The publisher has made every effort to trace copyright holders and welcomes correspondence from those they have been unable to contact.
A Library of Congress record exists under ISBN:

ISBN 13: 978-0-367-19931-9 (hbk)
ISBN 13: 978-0-429-24424-7 (ebk)

MERCANTILISM
AND THE
EAST INDIA TRADE

MERCANTILISM
and the
EAST INDIA TRADE

By

P. J. THOMAS

FRANK CASS & CO. LTD
LONDON

First published by P. S. King & Son Ltd.,
in 1926 and now reprinted by arrangement
with them.

This edition published by Frank Cass & Co. Ltd.,
10 Woburn Walk, London, W.C.1

First edition   1926

New impression 1963

Made and printed in Great Britain by
Charles Birchall and Sons Limited
Liverpool and London

PREFACE

THE object of this monograph is to trace the beginnings of Protectionism in England. Towards the last quarter of the seventeenth century, the Mercantile system became increasingly protectionist in aim, and this is disclosed by the numerous controversies that raged in the sphere of foreign trade at the time. The opposing views of Protection and Free Trade were clearly stated by a galaxy of talented writers, whom we may justly regard as the pioneers of modern economic thought. These controversies resulted in the triumph of Protectionism, and for more than a century it remained the settled economic policy of Great Britain. This early clash between Protectionism and Free Trade is only barely noticed in the existing books, but it deserves a prominent place in the history of economic development. The importance of this topic can only be brought out by segregating it from the general current of Mercantilism—by extricating it from that tangled web which has almost baffled analysis and has greatly confused the inexperienced student. This aim the present writer has kept clearly in view.

Of the many branches of English foreign trade, the East Indian was the one that figured prominently in the protectionist controversy, and hence the importance attached to it in this work. It must be noted, however, that the controversy was not between England and the East Indies, but between two powerful interests within England : the English woollen and silk manufacturers were pitted against the English East India Company and the English calico-printers. The subject is therefore essentially connected with England, and is only incidentally connected with India. It is a chapter—and an integral chapter—in the history of economic thought in general and of English economic development in particular. It is from this standpoint that the subject has been dealt with in the present work.

At a time like the present when there is a distinct revival of Protectionism in most countries, the subject of this treatise may be of special interest, not only to students but to statesmen. The safeguarding of " key " industries is

PREFACE

now recognised as a legitimate aim of State policy even in Great Britain, and few would now inveigh against such a policy. Nor was the object of the early protectionists essentially different from this. Most of them were genuine patriots who used the tariff policy as a weapon to defend national industries against unfair foreign competition, and who honestly held that those national industries should be safeguarded even against competition at home of new rivals ; they were not all craving for treasure or raving for national aggrandisement, as is often supposed. It is possible, therefore, that the early protectionist movement detailed in the present work may have some practical bearing upon the fiscal problems that loom so large all over the world at the present time.

The materials for this book were drawn mainly from contemporary papers preserved in the English libraries and archives—pamphlets, broadsides, and the teeming MSS. of the Public Record Office and the India Office. The period under survey was very prolific in economic tracts, and large numbers of them are found in the Bodleian, the British Museum and the Goldsmiths' Library of Economic Literature. The last-named collection was found specially useful : it is a veritable mine of economic information and awaits exploitation by enterprising workers.

The book was partly composed in 1922 and forms part of the results of an enquiry which the author carried on in the above archives from 1920 to 1924. It is proposed to bring out another instalment of his " findings " in due course.

The author takes this opportunity to express his deep debt of gratitude to the High Commissioner for India in London ; to Mr. P. E. Roberts, of Worcester College, Oxford ; to Prof. H. W. C. Davis, of Balliol ; to Mr. E. Lipson, University Reader in Economic History at Oxford ; to Mr. (now Sir) William Foster, Historiographer at the India Office, and to Mrs. V. Anstey, of the London School of Economics and Political Science. The publication of this book owes much to the munificence of Mr. T. C. Goswami, of Lincoln College, Oxford. The author's colleague, Prof. S. A. Pakeman, and Mrs. Anstey were good enough to correct the proofs, and the author is grateful to them both for their helpful suggestions.

P. J. Thomas, 1926.

PRINCIPAL SOURCES

I. MANUSCRIPTS

PUBLIC RECORD OFFICE :

Colonial Office 388.

Vols: 5 to 22, Original Correspondence of the Board of Trade, 1696—1720.

Colonial Office 389, Vols. 14 to 28 ; Entry Books, Reports, Instructions Orders, etc., from 1696 to 1731.

Colonial Office 77, Vols. 14 to 16. Petitions of the East India Company, etc. (1678-1725).

BRITISH MUSEUM :

Additional MSS. 10, 122. Parliamentary Grants, 1688-1702.

24B. Representations of the Commissioners for Trade and Plantations.

INDIA OFFICE LIBRARY :

Manuscript Letter Books ; Despatches to India, Commissions to Ships, etc. Vols. 7 to 17 (1682-1721).

Court Minutes—Minutes of the Court of Directors on all matters connected with the Company. Vols. 32 to 37 (1680-1700).

Abstracts of Letters from Coast and Bay. 2 Vols. 1703-1728.

Records of Fort St. George—Despatches from England. (Three volumes of Documents recently published by Government of Madras.)

GOLDSMITHS' LIBRARY :

India and the Far East MSS. Various accounts of Trade in the early Eighteenth Century. Contains Sir Nicholas Waite's " account of ye state of trade in India (1699)."

The Meanes of a most ample increase of the wealth and strength of England in a few years, offered to Queen Anne in the fifth year of her reign (1706).

BODLEIAN :

Rawlinson MSS. A. 303. Child's Letters, etc.

PRINCIPAL SOURCES

II. PARLIAMENTARY AND OTHER STATE PAPERS

Historical MSS., Commission Reports, New Series, 4 vols., the House of Lords Papers.
Journal of the House of Commons, Vols. XI to XX.
Journal of the House of Lords, Vols. XV. to XXII.
Bromley Papers (Petitions to Parliament.)
Treasury Papers.
State Papers, Domestic.

III. NEWSPAPERS (CONTEMPORARY)

The Old Weekly Journal; Weekly Journal or Saturday Post; Post Boy; Weekly Journal or British Gazetteer; Flying Post; Protestant Mercury; Weekly Packet; The Manufacturer; The Weaver; The British Merchant (1713); The London Gazette; The British Merchant (1719); The Mercator, or Commerce Preserved; The Spectator.

(Most of these are preserved in the Bodleian, especially in the Nichols collection.)

IV. PAMPHLETS

[The following is a list, chronologically arranged, of the pamphlets and broadsides preserved in the various libraries in London and Oxford.]

1623 Discourse of Trade to East Indies. (Thomas Mun.)
    The Circle of Commerce. (Misseldon.)

1664 England's Treasure by Forraign Trade. (Mun.)

1668. Brief Observations concerning Trade and Interest. (Josia Child.)

1677 England's Great Happiness, a Dialogue between Content and Complaint.
    East India Trade a most profitable Trade to the Kingdom.
    England's Improvement by Sea and Land. (Andrew Yaranton, Gent.) Two parts.

1678 The Ancient Trades Decayed and Repaired again.

1680 Britannia Languens. (Sir William Petty (?).)
    A Treatise concerning the East India Trade (Thomas Papillon.)

1681 A Treatise wherein is demonstrated that East India Trade is the most national of all Foreign Trades. (Child.)

1684 Colbert's Ghost.

PRINCIPAL SOURCES

1685 The English Interest. (Reynell.)
1690 A Jerk for the Jacks .
    A New Discourse of Trade. (Child.)
    Discourse on Trade. (Barbon N.)
1691 Political Arithmetick. (Sir William Petty.)
    A Discourse on Trade. (Sir Dudley North.)
    Considerations of the lowering of interest and raising the value of Money. (John Locke.)
    The Linen and Woollen Manufactory Discoursed.
1693 Observations on the Netherlands. (Temple.)
    Account of some transactions relating to the East India Company.
1694 An Abstract of the Grievances of Trade which oppress our Poor.
1695. Further Considerations. (Locke.)
    Angliae Tutamen.
    An Essay on the State of England relating to its trade, poor and taxes. (John Cary.)
1694 Tracts on Trade. (Cary).
1696 An Essay on East India Trade. (Charles Davenant.)
    The Naked Truth in an Essay upon Trade.
    A Letter to a Friend concerning East India Trade
    Discourse Concerning East India Trade. (Cary.)
    A Discourse of Trade, Coyn, Paper credit. (John Pollexfen.)
    Discourse on East India Trade. (Davenant.)
    England and India inconsistent with their Manufactures. (Pollexfen.)
    England's Danger by Foreign Manufactures.
    An English Winding Sheet for Indian manufactures.
    The Great Necessity of preserving our own manufactures. (N.C., Weaver of London.)
    Reasons for passing a Bill Prohibiting Silks, etc. (T.S., a weaver.)
    Prince Butler's case representing the wool case (a poem).
1697 Considerations on a Bill for Prohibiting East India Silks.
    The Great Honour and Advantage of East India Trade (Child.)
    The Linen Drapers' Petition.
    Answers to the Reasons against the Wearing
    The Linen Drapers' answer to Mr. Cary.

PRINCIPAL SOURCES

1697   A Reply to a Paper entitled, The Linen Drapers' answer to Mr. Cary. (Cary.)

Linen Drapers' rejoinder.

Fan Makers' grievance.

England's grandeur and the way to get wealth. (J. Tryn, Merchant.)

England's Advocate, in a letter to a Member of Parliament.

Querical Demonstrations. (" Prince Butler.")

Reply to a Paper delivered to Parliament. (John Cary.)

1699   A True Relation of the Rise and Progress of the E.I.Co., showing how . . prejudicial to the Manufactures of England.

Remarks on complaints against trade to East India as prejudicial to the Nation.

Discourse of East India Trade a Most Unprofitable Trade. (Cary.)

1700   England's Almanack showing that E.I. Trade is prejudicial to England.

England to be walled with gold and to have silver as plentiful as stones in the street, written for the good of the publick, by Joseph Coles.

1700   Case of Japanners.

A Letter to a Member of Parliament.

1701   Free holders' Plea against stock jobbing Elections of Parliament Men. (Defoe.)

The Considerations upon the East India Trade.

1702   True Interest and Political Maxims of Holland. (John de Witt (translated).

1704   Linen Manufactures in Ireland. (Cary.)

1705   Diseases of Tradesmen.

Art of Dyeing Considered.

Money and Trade Considered. (John Law, Edinburgh.)

1706   View of the Present State of Clothing Trade in England. (John Haynes.)

Considerations relating to Trade Considered.

Commerce and Navigation of the Ancients. (Huet.)

An Essay upon Industry and Trade.

1707   Interest of England Considered.

Decay of Trade and Credit.

Treaties on Moneys and Exchanges.

PRINCIPAL SOURCES

1708 Present state of Great Britain. (Chamberlayne.)

1709 Remarks on a pamphlet called "Reflections" of Dr. Davenant.

1710 Some reasons for a European State. (John Bellars.)

1711 Account of Trade in India. (Charles Lockyer.)

1713 Dr. Davenant's Prophecies.
Extracts from Several Mercators, being considerations on the State of British Trade.

1715 Provisions for the Poor and decayed state of Woollen manufactures. (John Haynes.)

1717 Ways and Means Discovered to enlarge Trade and Credit. A short but a thorough search.
Essay towards Regulating the Trade and Employing the Poor.

1718 Treatise on Regulating our Coins.
Survey of Trade. (Wood.)

1719 Weavers' Pretence Examined (by a Merchant).
A Brief State of the Question between Printed and Painted Calicoes and the woollen and silk manufactures.
Weavers' True Case. (Claudius Rey, a Weaver.)
Just complaints of the Poor Weavers truly represented. (Defoe.)
A Further Examination of Weavers' Pretences.
Brief Answer to a Brief State of the Question.

1719 Spinster in defence of the Woollen Manufactures.
A Short System of Trade. (David Clayton.)
An Essay on Trade, wherein the present dispute on calicoes also is considered.
Observations on Asgill's Brief Answer. (Rey.)
The State of the Question between Woollen and Silk Manufactures.
The True Case of the Scots Linen Manufacture.

1720 The Trade to India critically and calmly considered.
Elegy on the Death of Trade.
Linnen Spinster in defence of Linnen Manufactures.
The Female Manufacturers' Complaint.
The Spitalfields Ballad.
Observations on the Bill against the Calicoes.
The Interest of the Nation Asserted.
Weavers' Reply to the Linnen Drapers.

PRINCIPAL SOURCES

1720 Humble Address of the Weavers to the Ladies.
Stuff Weavers Case against Printed Calicoes examined.
Weavers' Twelve Queries.
Weavers' Twelve Queries answered.
Reasons for adding a Clause to the Bill against Calicoes.
The Languishing State of our Manufactures.
The Advantages of East India Trade considered.

1721 Memoirs, Life and Character of Mr. Law.

1725. The State of the Nation in respect of Coin, Debt and Money. (Erasmus Philip.)
Compleat English Tradesman. (Defoe.)

1726 The Importance of Ostend Company considered.

1727 A Brief Deduction of the Original Progress and immense increase of British Woollen Manufactures.
Atlas Maritimus Commercialis.
A Plan of English Commerce. (Defoe.)
Trade and Navigation of Great Britain considered. (Joshua Gee.)
Advantages of Peace and Commerce.

[The modern printed works utilized will be referred to in the footnotes.]

CONTENTS

CHAPTER I

MERCANTILISM IN THE SEVENTEENTH CENTURY

I

The Mercantile System

THE seventeenth century witnessed the birth of modern England. By the close of Elizabeth's reign, England had attained nationhood, and the struggle with the early Stuarts almost completed the process of unification. This was the achievement of the upper middle class which had grown in power and numbers under the social and economic influences of the fifteenth and sixteenth centuries, and it was to this class that power in the State passed when it was forfeited by the Crown. In 1649 they wrested sovereignty from the King, and in 1689 this transfer became more real with the accession of a royal house depending on Parliamentary tenure. The foundation of the British Empire must also be put to the credit of the same progressive class.

The predominant passion of the English nation when it came to its own was a stout patriotism which expressed itself in a rising sense of national solidarity and in an intense pride in English institutions. From the spacious days of Queen Elizabeth there had set in a rising current of national self-respect which carried the whole nation with it. After the Revolution of 1689 this current gained immensely in momentum. The literature of the period abounds in the most exuberant expression of this intense love of the motherland. " Great Britain," wrote Reynell, " is acknowledged by all the world to be the Queen of the Isles, and as capable to live within itself as any nation . . . . and is so incomparably situated that trade offers itself to all its ports and harbours."* " The Government of this nation," wrote Clayton, " is the best composed and best modelled of any that ever was in the world, so fitted for the happiness and freedom of all ranks and degrees of men that none but fools or knaves can find fault."† According to a third writer, the King of England (William III) was " the most potent prince of Christendom " ; " Cæsar, Pompey, Alexander and Hannibal must all resign their fame to him."‡ This growing spirit of patriotism found its most eloquent expression in that inimitable writer, Daniel Defoe, who asserted that England was " the greatest trading country in the world " ; that the English climate was " the best to live in " ; that Englishmen were " the stoutest and the best " ; that the tradesmen of England were " not the meanest of the people," and so forth in heroic strain.§ Another contemporary writer, Joseph Addison, expressed it in even stronger language when he wrote : " The meanest Briton scorns the proudest slave." This robust spirit was shared by the lower classes as well.

The national unity achieved was not only political, but even predominantly economic. The community of economic interests of the whole country was universally recognised long before 1689. A national economic policy had been growing in England ever since the days of Edward III ; under Elizabeth and the early Stuarts this was reduced to a system by the indefatigable labours of Lord Burleigh and other patriotic ministers. The new policy involved, on the one hand, increasing state regulation of industry and commerce ; and on the other, the replacement of the local and municipal autonomies of early days by a unified national policy directed by the central government for the benefit of the country as a whole. The one aim of this policy was

---

* *The True Interest of England* (1685), p. 1.
† *A Short System of Trade* (1719), p. 6.
‡ *A Jerk for the Jacks* (1690), p. 15.
§ *Compleat English Tradesman* (edition 1745), I, p. 241.

2

to enrich England and strengthen her against foreign aggression, and this was done by actively regulating and positively encouraging national industries and foreign trade. The sum-total of these regulations form what is called the Mercantile System.

Mercantilism has often been described as a definite and unified policy or doctrine, but that it has never been. In reality, it was a shifting combination of tendencies which, although directed to a common aim—the increase of national power—seldom possessed a unified system of policy, or even a harmonious set of doctrines. It was a very complicated web of which the threads mingled inextricably. Nor is it fair to the Mercantilist to identify his policy with the theory (once held as a dogma) of the Balance of Trade. The Mercantile System was by no means the outcome of the failure to distinguish between Wealth and Money. Various fallacies entered at various times into the kaleidoscopic shiftings of mercantile policy, but they were not of its essence. Individual mercantilists emphasised the need for bullion regulations, tariff barriers, navigation laws and the like ; but these were only various tendencies that came into prominence at various stages of mercantile policy. The core of mercantilism is the strengthening of the State in material resources ; it is the economic side of nationalism. The nation-state in its youthful enthusiasm sought to be powerful, and power was to be obtained by the growth of wealth in the country. Therefore the State protection of the material interests of the people was regarded as absolutely necessary. Schmoller hits the mark when he says that " state-making " is the innermost kernel of mercantilism. By state-making he means the creation of an economic community out of the political community.* And this was what mercantilism proposed to do.

Mercantilism was the dominant phase of England's policy, especially in the seventeenth and eighteenth centuries. It was the central government that wielded it, and local privilege was put down with a firm hand. The whole nation

---

* Schmoller, *The Mercantile System* (trans. Ashley), pp. 50-51.

looked to the State, not only for protection against foreign competition, but also for the regulation of conflicting commercial and industrial interests at home. Accordingly Government actively interfered in the details of economic life. The outflow of bullion was carefully regulated. Home industries were encouraged by providing for the importation of raw materials and by restraining the importation of finished products. The State also laid down from time to time the conditions of labour and employment in the various industries of the country. Nor were the interests of foreign trade neglected. Trading companies were incorporated under royal charter, and such companies received various privileges, including the monopoly of trade with distant territories. Trade was also fostered by navigation laws calculated to increase shipping, by the discouragement of harmful trades, and by a series of minute regulations in which the paternal State expressed itself.

For a long time the king kept the strings of economic policy in his own hands, but his authority was generally exercised under the advice of committees of experts set up from time to time. James I contemplated the creation of a Council of Trade, and Charles I actually instituted a Committee for Trade in 1626, on a more or less permanent basis, with instructions " to advance home commodities " and regulate trade and bullion.* This Committee did useful work till it was disorganised by the Civil War. It was revived by Cromwell, and was put on stable foundations by Charles II. In 1660, two bodies of experts were created for promoting the interests of trade and plantations respectively. These committees included prominent representatives of the trading companies as well as members of the Privy Council, and seem to have been very assiduous in promoting the economic interests of the nation. The functions of these two committees overlapped, and they were amalgamated in 1672 into a single body called the Lords Commissioners of Trade and Plantations. The Earl of Shaftesbury was the first chairman, and his "guide,

* Cunningham, *Growth of English Industry and Commerce* (Modern Times), 1907, pp. 175-6 ; also pp. 900-904.

philosopher and friend," John Locke, was secretary.* This board was composed of fourteen members, of whom six were unofficial paid members. The Commission's sphere of duties was very comprehensive, but concerned specially with currency, hindrances to trade, and employment of the poor. As a state agency for fostering trade and industry this body deserves unstinted praise. One cannot turn from even a cursory glance at their records without forming the highest opinions of their ubiquitous activity and their anxiety about even the minutest details of commerce and manufactures. Perhaps their policy was not always the wisest, but in everything they did the interests of the kingdom were consulted first and foremost.

Although the monarchical regulation of trade and industry was on the whole successful, Parliament became increasingly impatient ; and, from 1660, it asserted its right to wield an effective control over industrial and commercial matters. In 1689 the power of Parliament became practically complete, and the whole mercantile policy came to be wielded by it. There was necessarily a conflict of interests between Crown and Parliament, at any rate in foreign trade regulation. Kings used to impose customs duties on exports and imports, but this was primarily for the sake of revenue ; and naturally they were averse from imposing a high tariff lest it should diminish the volume of trade. But Parliament wanted to make use of the tariff to protect English industries, and even proceeded to prohibit some imports altogether. The king also was interested in protecting home industries, but was reluctant to pursue methods which entailed the reduction of his revenue.†
During Charles II's reign Parliament enforced its will repeatedly in the matter, and, after 1689, tariff policy came to be wielded mainly for protectionist purposes.

In the seventeenth century, the most active interference of the state was exerted in the sphere of foreign trade. There

---

* Cunningham, *op. cit.*, pp. 199-200 ; also pp. 913-921 ; see also Dict. Pol. Econ., Vol. I, p. 158.

† See, e.g., Charles II's opening speech in Parliament in 1679, *Parl. History*, IV, 1086.

was a strong tendency at the time to exalt foreign trade over domestic ; and the aim of Government was to regulate the course of trade in such a way as to enrich the country and foster its industries. All lines of foreign trade were judged good or bad according to the nature of their exports and imports. There were two distinct sets of formulæ for judging the profit and loss from foreign trade. If the imports from a foreign country were greater in value than the exports to that country from England, this would create an " overbalance " against England and in favour of that foreign country ; treasure would therefore flow into that country and impoverish England. If, on the contrary, England exported to that country more than she imported from it, trade would be favourable to England, because treasure would flow in to pay the balance, and would enrich the country. This was the gospel of Bullionism in the seventeenth century.

The other criterion concerned the nature of the exports and imports rather than their quantity or value. If trade involved the import of raw materials and export of manufactured goods, it was beneficial, because there would be more employment for the people. If, on the contrary, manufactured goods were imported and raw materials exported, employment would therefore be taken away from the people, and the country would be impoverished. This is the kernel of the protectionist view.

Of all lines of foreign trade, the East Indian was the one which caused the most acrimonious discussions in the seventeenth century. First, more commodities were imported from India than were exported to that country from England, and this caused that most dreaded of consequences—an unfavourable balance of trade. Secondly, the imports from India were increasingly of the nature of manufactured products which sooner or later were bound to displace home products and discourage home industry. Thirdly, the Company which carried on this trade under royal charter had a monopoly of the whole trade with extensive territories in the East, and by virtue of this monopoly excluded others from trading with those countries.

6

MERCANTILISM IN THE SEVENTEENTH CENTURY

There were also other minor charges against the East India Company. It brought into the country spices and other luxuries which caused great waste of national resources. Coffee, one of its imports, " served neither for nourishment nor for debauchery." The ship-building activity of the company caused a " parricide of woods," and made timber scarce in England. Many seamen died in its voyages to distant countries, and a multitude of widows and orphans were thus left by them. English ships, they said, could be employed more profitably in the coasting trade. The Company's organisation as a joint-stock concern was also severely criticised by other companies and by outside merchants. Questionable practices like stock-jobbing were from time to time laid at the Company's door. It was, besides, accused of artificially raising the prices and injuring the interests of both the tradesmen and the consumers.*

All these various charges against the Company and its trade produced heated controversies in the seventeenth and eighteenth centuries, and owing to the essentially economic character of these controversies, they became intimately connected with the main currents of economic policy and theory at the time. At least in the seventeenth century, foreign trade was the predominant concern of economic writers ; and the important position and unique character of the Indian trade was calculated to make it the main focus of economic thought as well as the vital concern of state policy. The pamphlet literature of the period under survey gives eloquent testimony to this fact.

Three principal controversies of the seventeenth century clustered round the three main charges against the Company enumerated above. The first two related to the nature of the Indian trade—i.e., the commodities imported into England ; while the third was concerned with the form of organisation of the Company. The first gave rise to the important discussion on bullion and the balance of trade, and directly led to the evolution of more correct economic notions on money and wealth, and on the nature of foreign

* These grievances are detailed in *Britannia Languens* (1680). ✓

7

trade. The second, viz., the onslaught against the importation of manufactured textiles from India not only gave occasion for the crystallisation of the protectionist doctrine of mercantilism, but also led to the birth of the opposite view of free trade. The controversy on the Company's monopoly did, in fact, greatly influence economic history inasmuch as the modern economic system of competition and free enterprise owed much to the protracted opposition against the Company in the seventeenth and eighteenth centuries. Although in the present work we are directly concerned only with the second of these controversies, the main lines of the other two may also be briefly sketched in this chapter.

II

The Balance of Trade Controversy

Indian trade has always been valued by foreign nations, but their appreciation of it was necessarily mingled with some apprehension about its baneful results. This was due to the peculiar character of Indian export and import trade. India always offered to the foreign trader valuable muslins and choice spices, but in return she took very few consumable commodities, and the result was that she had to be paid in gold or silver. It was thus that India came to be called " the sink of precious metals." As the English merchant, Terry, puts it : " Many silver streams run thither, as all rivers to the sea, and there stay."* The danger of a drain of treasure into India has been a perpetual nightmare to most of India's customers for the last two thousand years. The decay of the Roman Empire is imputed, at any rate partly, to this drain to the East.

From the very beginning of its trade connection with India, England had fears of a drain of specie, and stringent regulations were made as to the exportation of gold and silver by the East India Company. According to an Act of Edward III it was felony to export coin. Elizabeth's

* Quoted by W. H. Moreland, *India at the Death of Akbar*, p. 226.

charter, however, permitted the company for the first voyage to export Spanish or other foreign silver to the amount of £30,000, but in the case of subsequent voyages the company was obliged to " import within six months as much gold and silver as shall be equal to the value of the silver exported " by it.* But these restrictions were but feebly enforced, and in a few years' time the Company's bullion exports came to much higher figures. It was therefore found necessary to increase the Company's competence in the matter, and this was done by letters patent from the Crown in 1619, 1626 and 1628.†

With a view to preserving the treasure of the country and encouraging industry at home, it was provided that the Company should export English commodities to the East. Accordingly varying quantities of woollen cloth, iron, lead, quicksilver, cutlery and swordblades were sent to the Indian factories. There was, however, very little effective demand for these goods in India. The Company's iron and tin were too costly for the Indian consumer, and the other goods were wanted only in very small quantities. The company was particularly interested in opening a market in India for English woollens, but its efforts were attended with little success. The great majority of people in India wore only cotton clothing.‡ They might want a blanket or two, but equally suitable and cheaper goods for this purpose were made in India. Repeated orders were sent by the Company's directors to India urging the need for increased sale of woollens, and the factors in their turn worked hard to push on the business. But all these efforts were of little avail. The Dutch Company, however, achieved greater success. There were severe bullion restrictions put upon it, as upon its English compeer; yet that company always avoided the exportation of much gold and silver from Holland

---

* See Hunter, *History of British India*, Vol. I, p. 252. Sainsbury, Court Minutes, III, p. 267.
　† G. Birdwood, *Report on the Old Records of the India Office* (1891), pp. 263-264.
　‡ There is a common belief in India that cotton cloth protects one from cold better than woollen. There are amusing stories about it. See, e.g., Mukerji, *Art Manufactures of India* (1888), p. 342.

and cleverly managed to finance its Indian trade with the bullion gained in its dealings with other Asiatic countries.* Gold was obtained from China and Indo-China, and silver from Japan, and this obviated the need for carrying bullion from Europe. Subsequently the English Company also tried the same methods, and succeeded to a large extent in its object.

Much anxious thought was given to this problem both by the Company and by the Government. The Directors were advised by some ingenious people to conquer territories or plant colonies in the country in order to avoid sending there so much bullion, but this idea was then regarded " altogether impracticable in respect of a long voyage, the diseases to which our people are liable in those hot regions, and the Power, Force, and Policy of Most Indian nations."† Of course, this was in 1700, when Aurangzeb ruled as the head of a united empire.

Under such circumstances bullion was the principal commodity of export to India, and the products of English industries formed only an infinitesimal share of the Company's export trade. During the first ten years of its existence, the total exports of the Company amounted to £170,673, of which as much as £119,202 was bullion. In the next decade, the drain was even more marked, as has been admitted by Thomas Mun himself, one of the ardent promoters of the Company. Out of the total exports of £840,376 for the first twenty years of the Company's trade, only £292,286 was represented by goods ; and even these were in great part foreign goods.

Towards the latter part of James I's reign, there was great economic distress in England. Many causes contributed to this, but bullionists put it down entirely to the drain of money to India and other Eastern countries. All trading companies,—particularly the Indian—were vehemently attacked by pamphleteers like Thomas Milles‡ and Gerard Malynes,§ who put forward the bullionist view with great

* Moreland, *From Akbar to Aurangzeb*, pp. 59-64.
† *Some Thoughts on Ways and Means* (1705), p. 40.
‡ Chiefly in *Customers' Apologie* (1601) and *Customers' Replie* (1604).
§ *Canker of England's Commonwealth* (1601).

force. Although the attack was at first directed against the trading companies in general, it became gradually concentrated on the East India Company, owing to the pre-dominance that the Indian trade had gained among English commercial enterprises of the time.* Naturally, therefore, it fell to the Company to vindicate its trade, and in doing so it successfully questioned the truth of the popular doctrine of bullionism.

Owing to the gravity of the situation, James I appointed a Standing Commission of Trade in 1622 to suggest remedies for the grievances then existing. Among the terms of reference to this Commission was included the following : " Because the East India Company have been much taxed by many for exporting the coin and treasure of this realm, to furnish their trade withal ; or that which would otherwise have come in hither, for the use of our subjects, and that they do not return such merchandise from India as doth recompense that loss unto our kingdom." The Commission was therefore authorised to " enquire and search whether that Company do truly and justly perform their contract with us concerning the exportation, and by what means that trade which is specious in show may be made profitable to the kingdom." Yet the East India Company was strongly represented on the Commission, and had in it four of its principal promoters, of whom Thomas Mun was one.

The East India Company denied the charges levelled against it, and successfully maintained that its trade did not drain the treasure of the country, and even positively averred that it promoted national prosperity by its com-mercial operations. This was the thesis embodied in Mun's *Discourse of Trade to the East Indies*, published in 1621. The same conclusions were further expanded and stated with greater vigour and precision in his later works, *Petition and Remonstrance of the East India Company* (written in 1628 and published in 1641) and *England's Treasure by Forraign Trade* (published posthumously in 1664). These books of Mun not only silenced the bullionist attack against

* Yet the first defence of Company trading came from Wheeler, Secretary of the Merchant Adventurers, in his *Treatise on Commerce*.

the Company, but also developed a theory which came to be recognised as the very backbone of the Mercantile system. As we shall see later, this was not the only occasion when the defence of the East India Company brought about an advance in economic theory.

The attack against the Indian trade was based on the fallacious conception, noted above, that all trade must be judged profitable or otherwise to the kingdom, according as it gave rise to a favourable or unfavourable balance. That is, if a trade brought in money into the country it was profitable ; if on the contrary it involved exportation of money it was harmful, and must be suppressed. On this criterion, the East India trade was judged pernicious.

At the present time we should answer the above criticism by attacking the undue importance attached to treasure or bullion. Mun, however, recognised the value of bullion (although it would be untrue to say that he identified bullion with wealth), and was convinced that only a favourable balance—i.e., " making our commodities which are exported yearly to overbalance in value the foreign wares which we consume "—would bring treasure into the country. So far he agreed with the critics ; but he denied their two accompanying assumptions, viz., (i) that exportation of bullion was bad in itself ; and (ii) that trade with each country must be judged by its own separate balance. He maintained that without exporting treasure at the outset, additional treasure could not be had ; and he established the fact that the profit or loss to the nation should be judged by the *general* balance accruing to the nation rather than by the particular balance resulting from the trade with separate countries. This was his defence of the East India trade ; and this also supplied a fairly reasonable theoretical backbone to the Mercantile System.

A brief analysis of Mun's argument may be attempted here. Treasure could come into England only by foreign trade, for there were no gold or silver mines in the country. Without the export of bullion, profitable trade with the East was not possible, but this apparent loss was but the first step of a series which terminated with the importation of additional treasure into the kingdom. Mun gives an example : " If we send one hundred pounds into the East Indies to buy pepper there and bring it hither, and from hence send it to Italy or Turkey it must yield seven hundred thousand pounds at least in those places in regard of the excessive charges which the merchant disburseth in those long voyages, in shipping, wages, victuals, insurance, interest, customs, imposts and the like, all which notwithstanding the king and the kingdom gets." He draws an interesting analogy to this from the farmer's experience* : " If we only behold the actions of the husbandman in the seed-time when he casteth away much good corn into the ground, we will rather accompt him a madman than husbandman ; but when we consider his labour in the harvest which is the end of his endeavours we find the worth and plentiful increase of his actions." This analogy appealed to many, and greatly helped to make Mun's conclusions widely accepted.

Thus Mun's great argument was that although at the start England lost some treasure by the East India trade, it ultimately brought in much more treasure from other countries than was originally thrown away ; and that the unfavourable balance in the particular trade was therefore turned into a very favourable general balance for the kingdom. At about the same time, Edward Misselbon, who was also in the East India Company's employ, expounded practically the same views in his *Circle of Commerce* (1623).†

Mun defended the Company's trade not only because it resulted in an eventual influx of treasure, but also on other grounds. He showed that the Indian trade had increased the national wealth of the country, and strengthened its defences by promoting shipping, by training men for the naval services, by increasing the price of and export trade in wool and woollen cloth "' which doth improve the landlord's rents,' and finally by serving as a counterpoise to the ' swelling greatness ' " of Holland and Spain. It was boldly argued

---

* *England's Treasure by Forraign Trade*, p. 28.

† A year previously another work of Misselbon (*Free Trade, or the Means to Make Trade Flourish*) disapproved of the Company's bullion exports, but he recanted these views in the *Circle of Commerce*, published next year.

by him that the growth of English commerce and even her political greatness would rise or fall with the progress or decay of the Indian trade. This brilliant defence helped greatly to stave off the attack against the Company.

The theory of the balance of trade in this new sense became a generally accepted doctrine, and continued so for a long time. Not only merchants and writers, but statesmen became devoted adherents of it. According to Strafford, the overbalance of exports over imports was to be regarded as "a certain sign that the Commonwealth gained upon their neighbours." Cromwell also gave his assent to it, and emphatically stated it in his Act for the exportation of native commodities.* In 1665, Slingsby, who was for some time Master of the Mint, informed Samuel Pepys : "The old law of prohibiting bullion to be exported is and ever was a folly and an injury rather than good."†

Towards the close of the century, however, the soundness of the theory was questioned. Sir Josia Child, Charles Davenant and other writers were indeed prepared to admit that the general balance of trade was a more accurate criterion of profit or loss from foreign trade than the particular balances ; but they were not prepared to grant that the general balance itself was an absolutely sound test. Child, for instance, showed that the balance of trade arrived at by the calculation merely of exports and imports was bound to be inconclusive, owing to (i) the "difficulty and impossibility of taking a true account as well of the quantity as of the value of commodities exported and imported," ; and (ii) "the many accidents that fall out as losses at sea, bad markets, bankrupt(cy), also considerations, siezure, and arrests which fall out on several occasions."‡ Davenant also was suspicious of the value of the balance of trade theory. He wrote : "He that would compute with any good effect in matters relating to trade must contemplate the wealth, stock, product, consumption and shipping,

---

* See Hewins, *op. cit.*, p. xxx.
† Quoted by W. R. Scott, *Joint Stock Companies*, Vol. I, p. 267.
‡ *Discourse of Trade*, pp. 135-140.

as well as the exportations and importations of the country."*

No doubt these doubts concerning the sufficiency of the balance of trade doctrine were due to the deeper vision of these writers into complex economic phenomena ; but there was at the root of them also the fact that the usual calculations of the balance of trade had ceased to justify the East India Company. The exportation of bullion went on increasing, especially towards the close of the century, and by no manner of computation was it possible to show that there was a favourable balance for England from the Indian trade. Under such circumstances Child and Davenant, as supporters of the Company, were bound to drop the traditional appeal to the balance of trade. It is not implied that there was any hypocrisy in the attitude of these two great writers. They knew that there was an unfavourable balance for England ; and yet they also knew by various indications that England was becoming more prosperous. Their instinct, if not their reason, told them that the traditional view was not absolutely correct ; yet they did not know how to demonstrate its falsity. They were groping in the dark, and only dimly saw the distant light.

On the question of the nature of money also, economic opinion underwent change. No one, even in the seventeenth century, identified money with wealth. Although Mun attached great importance to treasure, he knew the true relation between money and wealth. To take only one passage : " Plenty of money in a kingdom doth make native commodities dearer which as it is to the profit of some private men in their revenues so it is directly against the benefit of the public in the quantity of the trade." Later writers like Barbon, Child and Davenant fully understood the true nature of money and its relation to wealth. Davenant laid it down that " Money is the servant of trade—at bottom no more than the counters which men in their dealings have been accustomed to reckon." *The Considerations upon East India Trade* (1700) knocked the bottom out of the old prejudice by the bold assertion that " The true and principal riches

* *Works*, I, p. 147.

whether of private persons or of whole nations are meat and bread and cloaths and houses and the conveniences and the necessaries of life. . . . These for their own sakes—money because it will purchase these are to be deemed riches ; so that bullion is only secondary and dependant ; cloaths and manufactures are real and principal riches."*

Nevertheless the old crude notions on bullionism and the allied conception of money persisted for a long time in the popular mind. They were appealed to in the attack against the French trade throughout the period from 1678 to 1713. In the matter of Indian trade, the bullionists did not make any virulent attack after the publication of Mun's books. Yet the preamble of the Act of 1699 prohibiting the importation of Indian silks and calicoes recounts the great detriment caused by the Indian trade to the treasure of the kingdom. The discredited doctrine of the balance of trade finally fell under the attacks of Adam Smith ; yet its influence can be traced up to the middle of the nineteenth century, and perhaps even later. Nor should it greatly surprise us that such a doctrine should be generally held in an age when the modern machinery of credit was unknown, and when exports and imports were necessarily a better criterion of the profit and loss from foreign trade than they have subsequently become.†

III

The Struggle against the Company's Monopoly

Throughout the seventeenth century, the protagonists of the East India Company convincingly argued that its trade was highly profitable to the kingdom. This came to be generally admitted in England, but this admission did not completely disarm the Company's opponents. On the contrary, the enormous gains amassed by the Company's

* See Chapter II.
† See Hewins, *op. cit.*, pp. 130-181. Also Marshall, *Industry and Trade*, p. 722.

shareholders raised the cupidity of the outside merchants and reared a class of interlopers who boldly poached in the Company's preserves. The whole nation watched with intense interest the rise and fall of the Company's stock; and the declaration of its annual dividends was awaited with impatience as much by business men outside as the shareholders within. The Company grew prosperous, and the outside merchants found no legal way of benefiting by that prosperity. The Company had a monopoly of trade with the whole East Indies; and no "outsider" could legally carry on trade with those regions. Similar monopolies were enjoyed by other Companies in regard to other territories. But there was this difference between the East India Company and the other trading corporations, that while the latter were founded as, and continued to be "regulated" associations of individual merchants each carrying on his own trade, the East India Company came to be organised as a joint stock corporation, and left little room for individual enterprise.* Besides, it was more difficult to get admission into the East India Company than into the regulated Companies. Thus that company became, in the words of Justice Pollexfen, ' an invisible body subsisting only in *intelligentia legis*, a body politic without soul or conscience.'

This was the standing grievance of the nation against the East India Company; and almost from its incorporation there arose a vigorous opposition which lasted for full two hundred years. The struggle became most bitter from the Restoration and culminated in the acrimonious scramble of rival companies towards the close of the seventeenth century. In 1708 the rival companies eventually united, but the outside merchants still kept up opposition and were pacified only when, in 1813, the monopoly of Indian trade was taken away from the Company. The struggle passed through many phases during those two hundred years and was fought in many lands and in many spheres. It was fought not only in England and India, but in the high seas

---

* The Company did not start as a *permanent* joint stock, but by 1657 became such. Until 1612, each voyage was managed by a separate jointstock. Subsequently the need for continuity was felt, and hence the change of 1657. See Hunter's *History of British India*, 2 vols.

all the world over. For a time it got mixed up with English party politics and clogged the wheels of State by its incessant outbreaks. Sir Josia Child had turned the Company into a ' Tory Corporation,' and naturally it had to suffer after the Revolution of 1688, when the Whigs came into power.*

What interests us in the present connection is not the dramatic character of the struggle—for this the reader may turn to the writings of Sir William Hunter or even of Macaulay—but its important effects on economic policy and thought. A protracted struggle went on in England throughout the seventeenth and eighteenth centuries against monopoly and State regulation ; and its outcome was the triumph of private enterprise and freedom of competition which were the dominant characteristics of nineteenth century economic life. The attack against the East India Company was one of the main currents of this momentous struggle. The Company was the stoutest champion of monopolistic trading and naturally the bitterest attack was directed against it. Its enemies were the ablest exponents of free enterprise (or " free trade " as it was then called) ; and its supporters wrote the clearest defence of trading monopoly. Adam Smith himself appeared as the champion of *laissez faire* as against monopoly and State interference ; and his relentless logic was feared by none so much as the Company.

A survey of this protracted struggle would require a whole volume if full justice were to be done to it. It is here proposed only to state briefly the main principles that entered into the struggle.

Monopolies of every kind are against the grain of English law and institutions, and whenever such monopolies were instituted, as by Elizabeth, James I, and Charles I, Parliament voiced the protest of the nation by an appeal to the " natural " right of freedom of trade or to the statutes of Edward III. Thus the " Free Trade " Bills passed in 1604, " scarce fourty voices dissenting," claimed that all merchants

---

* This question also introduced complications into the foreign policy of England. The British opposition to the Ostend Company is but one of many examples.

should have liberty of trade to all countries.* These were aimed mainly against the Merchants Adventurers and the Russia Company. After the Restoration, however, the same claim was made against the East India Company, by an overwhelming body of public opinion in England.

Nor was the East India Company rash enough to defend monopolies *in toto*. It always maintained that its claim to exclusive rights of trading with India was *sui generis*, rendered necessary by the great distance and unique nature of the countries with which it traded, and the peculiar dangers to which such trade was liable, and the difficulty of attracting sufficient capital except by offering such a privilege. Child and Davenant, although keen advocates of free trade (in the sense of immunity from tariff) were equally ardent supporters of the Company's monopoly. They pointed out various circumstances of the India trade which necessitated its management by an exclusive joint stock. The trade to East Indies involved diplomatic relations with heathen potentates; an adequate military force had to be kept up for defending trade and for suppressing piracy. These could not be managed by individual traders acting separately. "Nothing but a joint stock," wrote Davenant, "will produce such a joint force as might be able to preserve the traffic safe against pirates and foreign enemies in so long a voyage." On these grounds, too, the East India Company always claimed State protection for its monopoly.

These arguments hardly convinced anyone. It was admitted that there were special difficulties in the Indian trade, but as many writers pointed out, those could be got over by the Government directly establishing diplomatic relations with the Indian potentates, and keeping a navy or even an army in those distant regions.

Some very crushing economic objections were urged against the Company's monopoly by its opponents. It was injurious to English manufacturers, because being a monopoly it could dictate its own terms to them. It was also the interest of the company to sell raw products to the home

* *Commons Journals*, Vol. I, p. 218; also Eng. Econ. Hist. (Select Documents), pp. 443-453.

manufacturers at as high prices as possible. These high prices did injury to the nations, as it put too heavy a burden upon export trade. It was thus that the Dutch could outsell the English, but if trade were " free," prices would have fallen and the Dutch could have been ousted.

The remarkable pamphlet, *Britannia Languens* (1680), ably set forth the above and similar arguments against the Company's monopoly, and brought out the waste of economic resources involved in it. It showed how it was to the interests of the monopolists to cut down supplies rather than to reduce the price. They will " get more by selling a small quantity very dear than by selling much at a moderate profit."* Such monopolies also prevented the proper development of capital in the kingdom. " Though the joint stock employed be not sufficient to manage the trade anything near the full advantage, yet those interested in it will have reason to be satisfied with the return they make, since in proportion to the stock they may be very great ; and for the same reason may be contented to trade to a few ports where they can have great rates."† The pamphlet thus made a keen analysis of the nature of the monopoly and some of its views are very modern.

Throughout the whole struggle, all who favoured the East India trade also supported the monopoly. There was, however, one remarkable exception. The anonymous tract, *Considerations upon the East India Trade*, not only supported, as we shall see, the Company's free trade arguments but gave them a sounder setting. At the same time the writer vigorously attacked the Company's monopoly and was thus a consistent free trader. Under a monopoly, he pointed out, a few merchants gained most, but an " open " trade would benefit the whole nation. We shall have occasion to examine the contribution of this really "superior" tract to the economic thought of the period.

---

* This is indeed a weak point of monopoly, but such cutting down takes place only in the case of commodities the demand for which is not *elastic*, and the production of which does not come under the law of *Increasing Returns*.

† *Brittania Languens*, p. 133.

IV

The Protectionist Controversy

The latter half of the seventeenth century was the golden age of the Mercantile System. In the first half of the century the system was vitiated by an undue regard for bullion. The object of every patriotic writer and politician was to discover the easiest way of increasing the treasure of the land. As foreign trade was the means of bringing in gold and silver, its importance was exaggerated by both Government and the people ; and naturally state policy was directed towards the regulation of foreign trade with a view to bringing about the influx of treasure into the country.

Mercantilism entered a new and more remarkable phase towards the last quarter of the century ; and this phase continued in vigour during the greater part of the eighteenth century as well. The keynote of this policy was the fostering of national industries, and all the energies of the state were concentrated upon this main object. Indeed foreign trade continued to be as important as before, but it was valued, not so much for its own sake or the treasure brought by it, as for its effect upon home industries. The state came to regard it as its principal concern to regulate trade in such a way as to further industrial development. In the hands of a patriotic Parliament, this policy assumed the form of a vigorous protection of what were regarded as national industries against unfair competition from foreign countries. The foreigner was vigorously ousted, either by absolutely prohibiting his imports into England or by the milder method of protective tariffs. This phase of Mercantilism (which we might very well call *Protectionism*) was initiated in the interests of home industries, and was a clean and creditable movement so long as it looked to the collective well-being of the nation. But later it inevitably degenerated into a clash of rival interests at home ; and by its selfishness and greedy spirit exposed itself to the attacks of Adam Smith and other critics. When Mercantilism reached this last

C   21

phase, it was time for it to give place to the new policy of *laissez faire*.

The middle phase of Mercantilism above noted centred round the controversies that arose in connection with the French, Irish and Indian trades, and these struggles loom large in the economic history of that period. They were also formative influences of the first magnitude in the evolution of English economic thought. The protection of the principal English industries was the central idea of all these struggles, and they resulted in legislation of a predominantly protectionist character. Nor were they purely economic controversies ; political motives also got mixed up with some of them. And the issues were often confused by the many-sided character of the struggles.

The French trade controversy was a prominent political and economic question for a long period after the Restoration, and was not finally settled until the time of the younger Pitt. In 1678, imports of wines and brandies, silks and linens from France were absolutely prohibited by Parliament. After the accession of James II, a royalist parliament abolished this prohibition in order to please the king, but at the same time imposed high protective duties. In 1688, however, prohibition was re-enacted, and this remained in force till the conclusion of peace with France. In 1712, the controversy broke out again in connection with the free trade clauses of the Treaty of Utrecht ; and this was acrimoniously fought by the rival journals, *British Merchant* and *Mercater*.

The attack against the French trade was based mainly on the question of balance of trade. No doubt long-standing political and religious animosities embittered the struggle,* and there were also the interests of the English silk industry involved in it ; but it cannot be said that protectionism was the principal issue   The overwhelming " overbalance of at least one million pounds a year " in favour of France was detected by the merchants in 1674, and this alarmed the Commissioners for Trade and Plantations. This was

* The 'popery and wooden shoes' across the channel were then held in great derision in England.

also the main motive for parliamentary interference ; the question of protecting English industries was only a minor one. The principal French imports were wines and brandies, which hardly competed with English manufactures. The fear of a drain to France was predominant in the minds of the legislators. In 1677, Harbord cried out in Parliament : "Make a law to prohibit French trade ; you need no wine and few of his commodities ; and France will grow poor and you shall grow rich."* Besides the preambles of the chief bills on French trade put the exhaustion of treasure as the first and foremost danger against which Parliament wanted to guard the country.

The question of the Irish trade also came before Parliament in the last decade of the seventeenth century, and culminated in the stringent legislation of 1698 and 1699, prohibiting in perpetuity the exportation from Ireland of all goods made or mixed with wool, except to England ; and even this could only be done with the licence of the Commissioners of Revenue and on payment of a prohibitive duty. This enactment not only ruined the woollen industry of Ireland, but, according to various writers, proved ultimately injurious to the English woollen industry as well.†

The leading motive in the policy towards Ireland was no doubt the protection of English industries, but this was effected not by the usual method of restraining the importation of Irish goods into England, but by more direct methods ; and the question was dealt with more on political grounds than economic.

The Indian trade controversy alone was fought almost entirely on economic issues, and had little of political rancour underneath it. It is specially noteworthy that the economic issues raised by it centred mainly round protectionism, and partook little of the character of a bullionist struggle. It was concerned with the stopping of the unequal competition between the expensive home-made commodities and the cheap foreign goods, and thus the question was purely one of protectionism. It was the first controversy

* Parliamentary History, IV, p. 888.
† Alice Murray, *Trade Relations between England and Ireland*, pp. 60-65.

in which the protection of home industries was the predominant motive ; and it was fought on the now familiar lines of protection *versus* free trade. As might be expected, this first clash between these opposing policies broke new ground, and produced permanent results. It not only offered an occasion for clearing up the protectionist view (which was already familiar), but also led to the emergence of the opposing theory of free trade which (in its modern sense) was hardly known before. Hence the importance of this struggle to the student of economic history and theory, and the reason why it is treated in detail in the present work.

Dr. Cunningham calls this the New Attack upon the East India trade in contra-distinction to the old attack, which was concerned with bullion and balance of trade. This title may not be altogether unsuitable ; yet it would perhaps be better to make it more precise by giving it a qualifying epithet. Hence the phrase, " Protectionist Controversy " used at the beginning of this section. The New Attack was based on protectionism pure and simple, and this is its title to prominence as a topic in economic history.

Chapter II

THE INCREASED USE OF INDIAN TEXTILES IN ENGLAND

I
Change of Fashions

"Our ladyes all were set a gadding,
After these toys they ran a madding;
And nothing then would please their fancies,
Nor dolls, nor joans, nor wanton nancies,
Unless it be of Indian making."*

TOWARDS the middle of the seventeenth century, there was a remarkable change in the fashions of men's and women's clothes in England. The good old broad-cloth, ' the ancient glory of England,' had already been discarded, and even the finer fabrics of the new drapery were fast going out of use. The upper classes—and indeed the people generally—wanted light and elegant clothing. English weavers could not immediately meet this sudden demand, and naturally foreign stuffs were sought after. France stepped in to supply the need. Thus, in the words of the " judicious " Anderson, " the laudable English fashions of former times began to alter in favour of France. The women's hats were turned into hoods whereby every maid-servant in England became a standing revenue to the French king of the half of her wages."†

This was a time when French fashions and manners were universally admired ; and truly, France in the glorious days of the Grand Monarch was the unrivalled centre of civilisation. Charles II was an admirer of everything

* Prince Butler's Tale (1696 ?).
† Quoted by Macpherson, *European Commerce with India*, p. 334.

French, and readily copied the court-life of his pompous cousin across the Channel. The court set the fashion in those days, and naturally all respectable people followed suit. Just as French wine became 'a modish drink,' French silks and linens and other light stuffs came into everyday use in England. Clever dealers like D'Oyley seized this opportunity and catered for the new demand by importing these " sorry slight stuffs " from France* and adapting them for English wear. This produced a great commotion among English manufacturers and merchants, and the opposition party in Parliament (later called Whigs) took up the matter. In 1678 an Act was passed prohibiting French silks and linens, as well as wines and brandies. This was meant as a reply to Colbert's stringent arrét of 1667, prohibiting English cloth in France.

Although the new-fangled fashions of France were thus given up, the English people did not return to the use of their own woollens and silks. As a pamphleteer wrote, they were " no sooner prohibited the use of one foreign bauble but they fly to another."† This time they turned to far-off India " for the slightest, foolishest trash in the world, such as chintz,‡ slight silks, painted cottons, herba silk and no silk." " On a sudden," says the same writer, " we saw all our women, rich and poor, cloath'd in Callico, printed and painted ; the gayer and the more tawdry the better."

Another writer, as early as 1678, noted the same tendency. " Instead of green-say that was wont to be used for children's frocks," he wrote, " is now used *painted and Indian-stained and striped* calico ; and instead of a perpetuana or shalloon to lyne men's coats with, is used sometimes a glazened Calico which on the whole is not above 12d cheaper and abundantly worse." " And sometimes," he continues, " is used a Bengall§ that is brought from India both for

---

* *A Brief Deduction of the Original Progress and Immense Increase of Woollen Manufactures* (1727), p. 40.
† *Ibid.,* p. 50.
‡ Chintz is a printed calico.
§ Fine muslin from Bengal.

lynings to coats and for petticoats too."* About the same time, as we shall see later, the directors of the Company sent urgent orders to India for cotton goods of all sorts. Before this sudden change in fashion, only the poorest people used calicoes, and even that was for furniture and for " shrouds for the dead among those who could not go to the price of linen and yet were willing to imitate the rich."† But very soon it became the wear of the higher classes, " from the greatest gallants to the meanest cookmaids," so much so that one satirical writer said that it became difficult " to know their wives from their chambermaids." Another writer could not understand how this " ordinary mean, and low-priced " thing could become the wear of the " gayest ladies on the greatest occasions."‡ The Company noted this change immediately, and was partly responsible for it. They made presents of the best Indian muslins to ladies in high position—an act that called forth abundant satire against its authors. In 1687 the directors wrote that " the calicoes and chintzes had become the wear of the ladyes of the greatest quality, which they wear on the outside of gowns and Mantuas which they line with velvet and cloth of gold."§

Some writers would have it that Queen Mary II was the first " to set the fashion of using chintz and East India Calicoes in dress,"‖ but long before this, persons in high life had taken to such clothing. Her luxurious uncle, Charles II, had a fancy for outlandish things, and so had the numerous ladies of his Court. It is true, however, that the new fashions came to be widely adopted under William and Mary. Mary's published letters have confirmed the verdict that she was one of the most fascinating characters of her age, and was the very flower of Stuart womanhood. She had high æsthetic tastes, and took delight

---

* *The Ancient Trades Decayed and Repaired Again* (1678), p. 16.
† Cary, *A discourse of Trade Concerning East India Trade.* Pollexfen, *Discourse on Trade.*
‡ *Brief Deduction* . . . (1727), p. 50.
§ India Office, MS. Letter Books, VIII, p. 275.
‖ Mary Bateson in *Social England,* IV, p. 828.

in collecting Eastern ornaments and the wonderful products of the Indian loom. According to Defoe, " Her Majesty had a fine apartment (at Hampton Court) with a set of lodgings for her private retreat only, but most exquisitely furnished, particularly a fine chintz bed, then a great curiosity."* Queen Anne too had a distinct taste for artistic things, and led the fashion in her time. Defoe expressed it plainly in 1708 : " Even the Queen herself at this time was pleased to appear in China and Japan, I mean in silk and calico."† The predominance of these new modes in England may be studied in the carpets and decoration of the period.

The numerous pamphlets of the time are full of satirical remarks about the increased use of Indian calicoes and chintzes.‡ One author, supposed to be Steele, wrote : " Their great-grandmothers, who for ornament and dress painted their own bodies, would be astonished at the Calico-picts, their degenerate children, and fly from their own offspring."§ Another said : " lite commodities are always most encouraged by lite women ; *similis simili gaudet*."‖ A third writer declared that those light commodities were " as light as women and as slight as cobwebs." " Fashion is truly termed a witch,"** said a pamphlet of 1696; "the dearer and scarcer any commodity the more the mode ; 30 shillings a yard for Muslins, and only the shadow of a

---

* Quoted by Lenyfon, *Decoration in England*, 1660-1770, p. 215.
† *Weekly Review*, 1708.
‡ Even classical writings of the seventeenth and eighteenth centuries mention chintz and other Indian cloths. See, for instance, Pope, *Moral Essays*, I, 248 (*circa* 1733) :
"No, let a charming chintz and Brussels lace
 Wrap my cold limbs, and shade my life-less face."
Elsewhere :
"And, when she sees her friend in deep despair,
 Observes how much a Chintz exceeds Mohair."
See also Crabbe, *Rejected Addresses* :
"Like Iris' bow down darts the painted clue,
 Starred, striped, and spotted, yellow, red and blue,
 Old calico, torn silk and muslins new."
§ *The " Spinster " in Defence of the Woollen Manufactures* (1727), p. 16.
‖ *Interest of Britain Considered* by J.B. (1707).
** Brit. Mus. 816.M. 12, No. 15.

commodity when procured."* An amusing story was told of an Indian boy at Leadenhall Street saying to another Indian boy (whom he calls Pompey !) : "there is nothing in this country that excell those of ours except it be that they are governed by their wives." "They go to our country," he adds, "to bring home to their women fine dresses from head to foot, only to purchase of them their hair for Periwigs."† And so on *ad nauseam*.

The extent of the use of Indian goods may be more or less estimated from contemporary writings. Cary,‡ Defoe and other writers give us a vivid idea of the changes. Men used shirts, neckcloths, cuffs and romals§ (handkerchiefs) made of calico ; and women had head-dresses, night-rails,‖ hoods, sleeves, aprons, gowns and petticoats made of Indian cloth. Both sexes wore Indian stockings. Dressing-gowns came to be generally made of calico. The lists of stolen goods mentioned in documents of the day included Kincob** gowns, Allejah†† petticoats, yellow chintz gowns and petticoats, muslin lace night cloths and other Indian names.‡‡ In 1698, according to George Chalmers, every lady was all the morning in muslin night-rails, and made and received visits in that dress. Ruffles both of gentlemen and ladies were of muslin.§§ Men wore large neckcloths of muslin. We read of a "cluster of high class ladies appearing like an embassy of Indian Queens." And it was no wonder at

* *The Naked Truth in an Essay upon Trade*, p. 11.
† *The "Spinster" in Defence of the Woollen Manufactures*, p. 16.
‡ Cary, *Disocurse of Trade Concerning East India Trade*, p. 5.
§ "Romal" is from the Persian Rūmāl, which means a towel or kerchief. This was much used in England at the time. It came chiefly from the Madras coast.

‖ This word is now rather obsolete. A night-rail is a "loose wrap," dressing jacket or dressing gown, as worn by women when in undress " (Oxf. Dict., Vol. VI).

** Gold brocade (formerly Camonoca, *Persian*), Hobson-Jobson, p. 484.

†† A silk cloth, originally from Turkestan ; also occurs as Alaji, Elatche, etc. (Hobson-Jobson).

‡‡ Ashton, *Social Life in the Reign of Queen Anne*, p. 167. Compare these with the names of cotton goods given in Hobson-Jobson.

§§ MS. *Essay on Balance of Trade* (1698-1719), by G. Chalmers (Public Record Office), C.O. 390, Vol. 14, p. 53 *et seq*. "Ruffles at the wrists were formerly an ordinary appendage of male costume " (Oxford Dictionary). So also were neckcloths.

that time, since the Queen and the ladies of the Court appeared in muslin and calico.

The chief Indian cotton goods popular at the time were muslins, chintz, calicoes, diapers, dimities and so forth. Most of the numerous varieties mentioned in the Company's records figure also in contemporary literature and correspondence. Ashton mentions also, among others, Baft, Beteele, Dorea, Palempore, Salempoory, Romal, Nillae, Mooree, Izaree, Anjengo calico.* All these were well known to the fashionable people of those days.

Indian calicoes were used for beds, screens, hangings,† and for covering cabinets and other furniture. In fact it was from these that they were later on promoted to the bodies of men and women. As Defoe satirically put it, " the chintz was advanced from lying upon their floors to their backs, from the footcloth to the petticoat."‡ The extensive use of Calico on furniture is well brought out by the same writer. " It crept into our houses, our closets and bed-chambers ; curtains, cushions, chairs, and at last beds themselves were nothing but Callicoes or Indian stuffs." " In short," he concludes, " almost everything that used to be made of wool or silk, relating either to dress of the women or the furniture of our houses, was supplied by the Indian trade."§

Nor was England the only country in Europe where Indian cotton and silk goods were used. They were introduced and were increasingly worn all over the continent. In France, their use spread like wild fire, and the local silk and linen industries were greatly harmed by this change. Colbert's arrét of 1686 checked this for a time, but it by no

---

* His list is given in his work, p. 178. *Baft* or *Bafta* is a kind of calico made specially at Broach ; *Beteele*, a kind of muslin (Spanish, *Beatilla*), *Dorea* is striped cloth ; *Palempore* and *Salempore* are two kinds of chintz, from Madras coast ; *Nillae* is blue cloth, and so also is *Moorie* ; *Izaree* means a kind of drawers or trousers (Hobson-Jobson).

† MS. Letter Book VII, 1682.

‡ *Weekly Review*, Jan. 31, 1708.

§ It is also noteworthy that the Indian designs on chintzs were imitated by English embroiderers and potters in the 18th century. (See Birdwood, The *Arts of India as illustrated by the Prince of Wales' Collection, passim.*)

means did away with the use of Indian calicoes and muslins. These Indian goods were commonly used also in Germany, Spain and Italy. Much calico went to Spain from England, and the Custom House records contain certain accounts of the exports from 1697.* According to Daniel Defoe,† Calicoes were sent from India " by land to Turkey, by land and inland seas to Moscovy and Tartary and about, and by long sea into Europe and America." This account is confirmed by other contemporary pamphlets.‡

II

Indian Textile Manufactures

It will be necessary to explain how it was that India which to-day imports a great deal of her clothing from England, managed to export into that country such large quantities of cotton and silk goods in the seventeenth century. To those who are unacquainted with the economic history of India—which is still a sealed book to most—this must appear rather strange and inexplicable. The explanation is that the economic functioning as well as the industrial structure of the various parts of the world have undergone most far-reaching changes since the Industrial Revolution.

When British commerce was established with the East early in the seventeenth century, India was the unrivalled centre of cotton manufactures in the whole world. What silk was to China, linen to Egypt, wool to England, that was cotton to India. Indian control of cotton and cotton goods amounted almost to a monopoly from very early times right down to the nineteenth century. As the *Atlas Maritimus* (1727) pointed out, India and China were able to clothe the whole world with their manufactures. This industry was carried on all over India by craftsmen, but

* Public Record Office, C.O.77, No. 16.
† *Plan of Commerce* (1728), p. 80.
‡ See, for example, *Advantages of Peace and Commerce* (1727) ; *Atlas Maritimus* (1727)—*passim*.

when the Industrial Revolution in England cut down the cost of production and facilitated the processes of spinning and weaving, Indian industry necessarily lost ground, and the foreign markets of India were lost. Although faced by a grossly unequal competition, the Indian manufactures dragged on their existence for a long time, and until quite recently, Indian muslins were exported into England and commanded high prices there.

The cotton industry of India is astoundingly ancient. Indian cloth was known to, and used by, the Egyptians, Babylonians, Persians, Greeks, Romans and other civilised peoples of antiquity. At the beginning of the Christian Era, Græco-Roman traders carried on a brisk commerce in choice Indian muslins and chintzes. India supplied a large proportion of the elegant costumes worn by the fashionable ladies of Rome and other cities of her extensive empire. In the middle ages the Arabs similarly carried Indian cloths to the ends of the earth. The peoples of Japan, China and Indo-China also used to wear them from early days.

The bulk of Indian cotton goods consisted of calicoes,* either plain or coloured, which were used for ordinary wear, and these were produced in most parts of India. Printed calico (called chintz) was much more valued for its elegance and beauty; the country around Masulipatam had had from early days a practical monopoly in its production. In the Middle Ages, according to Marco Polo, " Masulipatam produced the finest and most beautiful cottons found in any part of the world."† The best cotton cloth is " muslin," and this mostly came from Bengal.‡ Even in the Roman times, the lower valley of the Ganges specialised in the most beautiful muslins, called " Gangetica " in the *Periplus*. It is remarkable that this localisation of industry which the

---

* The word calico originated from Calicut, the Malabar town from which it was exported to Europe, but Calicut was never a centre of calico manufacture.

† *Travels*, Bk. III, ch. 21. Tavernier too gives prominence to Masulipatam, Bk. VIII, ch. 13.

‡ *Muslin* is derived from Mosul, on the Tigris, although all muslin came from India.

USE OF INDIAN TEXTILES IN ENGLAND

Romans noted in the first century has been kept up until quite recent times. The silk manufacture of India is also of long standing, although not so ancient as cotton. Long before the arrival of European traders, there was an important silk manufacture in the country. Kasimbazar (Bengal) specialised in this industry, and under the fostering care of the early East India Company, this industry prospered to such an extent as to compete successfully with China. Brocades, silk carpets and other stuffs were made also in Ahmedabad, Benares, and other places.*

The widespread use of Indian textiles is amply explained by their astounding excellence. Writers of every age wax eloquent when they speak of the quality of Indian muslins. It was their lightness, elegance and fine texture that made them always dear to the fashionable people in every country. According to the French traveller, Tavernier, without doubt a competent judge of such commodities, "some calicoes are made so fine that you can hardly feel them in your hand, and the thread when spun is scarce discernible."† "When a man puts it on," he says elsewhere, "his skin appears as plainly as if it were quite naked."‡ Amusing stories are told in India of the wonderful transparency of Indian muslins. The Emperor Aurangzeb was once angry with his daughter for showing her skin through her clothes; whereupon the young princess remonstrated in her justification that she had seven jamahs (suits) on. As some writers have pointed out, when such thin muslin is laid on the grass and the dew has fallen on it it is no longer discernible. It was of such cloth that Baines, in his famous *History of the Cotton Manufacture*, speaks that they "might be thought the work of fairies or of insects rather than of men."§ No wonder that such muslins are still prized more than the masterpieces of the most modern Manchester factory.

There are various ingenious ways of testing the

* See Prof. J. Sarkar, in the *Modern Review*, June, 1922, p. 678.
† *Travels*, Vol. I, p. 811.
‡ Vol. II, pp. 4-6.
§ *History of Cotton Manufacture* (1835), p. 56.

excellence of muslins. Even a long piece twenty yards long and one yard wide is expected to pass through a wedding ring. Another method of testing muslin is by taking its we'ght. The best piece of muslin, at least fifteen yards long, is supposed to weigh only a tenth of a pound. A Persian ambassador, returning from India in the seventeenth century, p .sented his royal master with a cocoanut set with jewels, containing within it a muslin turban thirty yards long. But such excellence has long passed away, and is not even attempted at the present time.*

Some of the poetic names of muslin tell their own tale. " Subnam " (or evening dew) is the name for a thin pellucid variety, because it is scarcely distinguishable from the dew on sand. Another of the *chefs d'œuvres* of Dacca is called *Abravan* (running water) because it is supposed to be invisible in water. " Alaballee " (very fine), " Tanjeb " (ornament of the body), " Kasa " (elegant) are also interesting examples of poetic nomenclature. These goods were called by similar fanciful names in other countries also. It has been called in Europe *ventus textilis* (textile breeze) 'web of woven air,' 'cobweb,' and so forth. The woollen manufacturers of England said that muslin was the shadow of a commodity rather than a commodity by itself. This was indeed great praise.

The chintz also has always been appreciated by India's customers all the world over. Expert critics have heaped unstinted praise on the delectable designs and the wealth of floral forms which characterise the Masulipatam Chintz. According to Sir George Birdwood,† their flowering is " perfect alike in poetry and technical skill," and the flowered chintz is " animated with a soul of its own and betters all those who look upon it."

Yet these ravishingly beautiful cloths were woven and printed by a simple folk in their own humble dwellings with the aid of a few crude tools. They had no accurate scientific

---

* This industry is now practically dead. The Exhibition at Wembley (1924) has only one old specimen of the old Dacca work.

† *The Arts of India as Illustrated by the Prince of Wales' Collection*, p. 80. See also G. P. Baker, *Calico Printing and Painting in the East Indies* (1921), *passim*.

knowledge, nor had they any elaborate machinery. They were often unlettered, unostentatious craftsmen and did not earn more than a penny or two a day. It was this aspect of the Indian manufacturers that specially struck Baines.* "It cannot but seem astonishing," he wrote, "that in a department of industry where the raw material has been so grossly neglected, where the machinery is so crude, and where there is so little division of labour, the results should be fabrics of the most exquisite delicacy and beauty unrivalled by the products of any other nation, even those best skilled in the mechanical arts."

Nevertheless, the conditions were not so simple as Baines supposed. No doubt the craftsman usually worked in his house, but he belonged to a guild which jealously guarded the traditions of the industry and he usually worked for a clothier (Mahajan) who supplied him with capital and undertook the marketing of his products. Besides, although the craftsmen (at least the bulk of them) lacked literary culture, they had nevertheless a highly specialised technical training which was rendered the more effective by the potent influence of heredity. The relation of the craftsman to his family, caste, and guild (which was generally distinct from caste) accounts for the admirable industrial organisation that obtained in India in early days.† Besides, the craftsmen had always a respectable place in the Indian social organism, and they still retain that position in certain parts.

In spite of their remarkable excellence, the Indian textiles have always been cheap, and this made them popular in other countries. It was the low standard of living and low wages obtaining in India that made this possible. Indeed, wages were low, but it was not because "the people in India are such slaves as to work for a penny a day" (as Colonel Birch said in the House of Commons in 1680) ‡ but because the climate of the country and the mode of life are such as to enable people to have a comparatively low standard of living ;

---

* *op. cit.*, p. 56.
  † See, for a description, the author's paper in the *Modern Review* (Calcutta), February, 1924.
  ‡ See *A Collection of Papers relating to the East India Trade* (1730), p. 81.

and besides, the penny a day was even in those days worth much more in India than in England. Certain contemporary pamphlets show a better insight into the question. According to one of them,* " Indians and Chinese are a numerous and laborious people, and can and do live without fire or clothing and with a trivial expense for food." Even the French craftsmen of the time, according to these pamphleteers, " scarcely cut flesh four times a year," and accepted low wages. But the English workman "will not work under a shilling."† This difference in the standard of living between the various countries was then one of the difficulties that stood in the way of unfettered trade between them.

III

English Import Trade in Indian Textiles

When trade relations were first established between England and India, cotton and silk goods did not figure prominently in the import trade. It was for competing with the Dutch in the matter of the pepper trade that the East India Company was formed in 1600 ; and for a long time pepper and other spices constituted the main items of importation into England. However, Indian calicoes and muslins were already known in England, ‡ and the Company from the first brought in small quantities of such goods to satisfy the home demand. Entries of calicoes are found in the Company's records from 1602.§ In 1620, fifty thousand pieces of calico were imported, and in 1634 the figures rose to 100,000.‖ Yet for a long time this trade remained a mere " side-line " of the Company's business.

* *An English Winding Sheet for Indian Manufactures* (1698), p. 1.
† *Ibid,* cf. Knowles, *Industrial and Commercial Revolutions,* Part II, *passim.* Also Gray's *Debates,* Vol. III, p. 430.
‡ It was first brought into England, perhaps by the Genoese ; at any rate the Portuguese must have introduced it. Calico is mentioned by Dunbar (1505) and by Draper's Dictionary (1578). See Oxf. Eng. Dict., II, p. 32.
§ Sainsbury, *Court Minutes,* I, p. 135.
‖ For the early history of the Company's calico trade, see Moreland, *From Akbar to Aurangzeb,* pp. 123-34.

USE OF INDIAN TEXTILES IN ENGLAND

From the first, this trade in textiles was regarded as a profitable one, because the Company disposed of the goods at three and even four times their cost price. In 1602, calicos bought at 4s. were sold at 12s. a piece, and in 1620, a seven-shilling piece brought 20s. to the Company's treasury. At the same time, there were misgivings in the minds of many that the new trade would ultimately turn out detrimental to English industries. Even Thomas Mun, ardent supporter of the East Indian trade as he was, thought that it was not profitable for the state of Christendom in general. In another way, however, calicoes were found advantageous : they " served to abate the excessive price of French linen " then being imported into England. In 1623, the Deputy Governor of the Company, accompanied by Mun, interviewed James I, and when the inquisitive king asked " what vent they had for the mass of the callicoes that came yerelye," they answered "that much was used in England whereby the price of lawns and cambrics were brought down." " For the rest," added they, " England is now made the staple for this commoditie." The king approved exceedingly thereof and said that this was the ready way to bring treasure into the kingdom.* Nevertheless, this trade did not show any great increase, partly owing to disturbances in India and partly also to the stationary nature of the demand in England.

From about 1670, however, Indian calicoes and silks were imported into England in larger quantities. Even from 1665 we find in the Director's despatches a distinct note of preference for these goods ; and this went on increasing year after year until it reached its acme in the years 1680-82. It was about that time that Indian cotton and silk goods came into fashion in England.† French linens and silks were stringently prohibited in England, and this too contributed to increase the demand for Indian fabrics. In 1684, when James II came to the throne, Parliament in a fit of loyalty to the crown, abolished the prohibition ; but heavy duties were imposed on French goods in order to

* W. Foster, in the *Journal of the Royal Society of Arts* (1918), p. 365.
† See last section.

enhance the king's customs revenue. The import trade with France staggered under the blow, and did not revive even after 1684. After 1688 French goods were again prohibited, and this was the East India Company's opportunity.

The results of the above advantage may be studied in the Directors' despatches to India. The lists of goods to be provided annually had been hitherto made up chiefly of saltpetre, indigo, pepper and other commodities ; but after 1678, textile goods of various kinds almost monopolised the space on the list ; indigo and the spices were relegated to a corner.* The despatches also breathe an entirely new spirit of optimism. The Directors wrote in 1682 ; " You may observe that our methods are changed, and we have got out of our old beaten paths ; our ships are coming to you at all times." Calicoes had, they said "become the wear of the ladies of the greatest fashion."† They prohibited their servants from trading in silks and calicoes on their own private account, and insisted on " having the markets in England entirely to the Company." The increasing prominence of the calicoes is also evident from the most minute details given of the colour, designs, and the exact shape of flowers needed for the goods ordered.

The Company had already a well-regulated establishment for trading in textiles. Its three principal factories then— Madras, Hughli and Surat—were in the heart of the three cotton manufacturing regions of India ; and each of them had an expert staff to deal in them. Nor were such arrangements confined to the three presidency towns. Below them were subordinate " factories " all over the country to deal directly with the producer. Around Dacca, even petty villages had their *aurang* or small warehouse. These mofussil establishments were managed by a clerk with the help of Dalals (or brokers) and a cloth expert (called Jachandar). The Company employed artisans by offering liberal advances of money and provisions according to the custom of the country.‡ They were also given full freedom of worship

* See Appendix A.

† Letter Books, VII, p. 154.

‡ See, for a description of the system, the author's paper in the *Modern Review* (March, 1924).

within the Company's walls ; and this was at a time when religious tolerance was hardly recognised in England.

The Company not only urged the authorities in India to encourage workmen and increase their production for export ; it did everything in its power to advance the industries of India. In this direction it was pushed on to lengths not justified by current views on patriotism. The Directors sent out patterns and models of piece-goods from England in order to instruct Indian weavers and printers as to the sort of goods wanted in England. More than this : they also sent to India some artificers to teach Indian artisans English modes of weaving and dyeing. Examples of the former can be met with in the Letter-Books of the Company. Almost every year fresh patterns were sent to India to guide Indian workmanship.* In 1680, the Company sent to Madras two hempdressers, two spinners, and a weaver that they may " put them into the way of making such hempen sailcloth as this Kingdom is usually supplied with from France and Holland."† In 1682, a mercer was sent to the Bay to mix colours for silks at Kasimbazaar.‡ In the same year dyers and throwsters were sent to Bengal. In 1683 the Company at home tried to induce flaxdressers to go to India but they would not go, " being an inland sort of people and not used to travel out of England."§ In 1684, John Hilman, a weaver, was sent to Bengal. He was entered in the books as a soldier because there were then complaints in the country against the Company's indiscretions.

The woollen and silk manufacturers violently attacked the Company for sending English artificers into India, and made this a principal count of the charge against it in Parliament in 1696 and 1699. The Turkey Company also blamed the sister Company for sending dyers to India and thereby ruining the Turkey trade. Many tracts and broadsides exposed the folly of Englishmen in thus helping the heathen

---

* e.g., Patterns of Hangings sent to Bay, April 23rd, 1683.
† Records of Ft. St. George, 1680-82, p.21. Edited by H. Dodwell.
‡ Letter Books, V, p. 59.
§ Letter, October 1st, 1683.

subjects of the Great Moghul. *An English Winding Sheet for Indian Manufacturers* has the following interesting words on the subject: "It was the English that sent over artists to all these trade and pattern-drawers and patterns that might suit the European humours . . . Indians could not do less than laughing in their sleeves . . . . It *was* the English, it *is* the English, it *will be* the English that will be the mad part of the world in this respect."*

This charge against the Company was certainly exagerrated as it was bound to be under the circumstances. Indian artisans were not influenced to any appreciable extent by this "mad enterprise" of the Company.

The patterns sent were generally goods taken home from India by the interlopers and other private traders and do not seem to have influenced the artisans in any other sense than indicating to them the goods proper for the English market, i.e., what kind of flowers and stripes were in fashion at the time in England, and so forth. And Indian workers were always on the alert to adapt their art to the needs of foreign markets. This readiness on their part is evident from the foreign designs on chintzes and other devices put in order to please European customers. Anyhow the Company soon recognised the folly of curtailing the liberty of the Indian artificers, and instructions were repeatedly sent to India to leave all details of work to the unchecked imagination of Indian workers. As early as 1683, the Directors wrote to Bombay: "Let your weavers take out such flowers most convenient and agreeable to their own fancies which will take better here than any strict imitation which is made in Europe." In 1697, they again wrote in the same strain to Bombay, but in even stricter language. Such instructions were repeated many times as when in 1731 it was definitely laid down: "Let the Indians work their own fancies, which is always preferable before any patterns we can send you from Europe."

Observe also that the artificers who went to India either did little there and were soon recalled, or they set up as private

* See also *A True Relation of the Rise and Progress of the East India Company* (1699), and other tracts.

craftsmen. In 1687, The Directors wrote to Bengal : " We have found by long experience that dyers and throwsters in Bengal are a great expense to the Company and work but very little for us. . . . Therefore we desire you to recall them to the Fort and send them home from hence." We may note also that the artificers sent were chiefly for linen manufacture. In the technique of cotton weaving and printing, Indian craftsmen were far in advance of the rest of the world at that time.

IV

Increase of Import Trade in Calicoes

As a result of the manifold circumstances detailed above, the Company's textile trade increased marvellously during the last two decades of the seventeenth century. The Letter-Books of the Company offer a profitable study during this period. In 1678, the year in which according to *England's Almanac,* ' muslins, beat out cambrics and lawns,' 10,000 pieces of ginghams*, as many of humhums† and cossæs‡, and 4,000 pieces of malmuls§, along with other minor items, were ordered from India. From 1682 the quantities ordered mount up to even higher figures. In that year‖ Surat alone was asked to supply 333,600 baftas of various kinds, 173,000 chintzes of many sorts, 90,000 tapseils,** 51,000 nicarees, 110,000 pautkas, 18,000 dungarees†† and 23 other different varieties of piece goods in lesser quantities. The total goods that Surat alone had to supply were 1,407,800 pieces of various kinds. From the Fort, 1,273,000 pieces of different sorts were asked for in the same year. The demand for Bengal goods was not then so

* *Gingham* is a mixed stuff, mostly cotton.
† " A cloth of thick, stout texture " (from Arabic *Hammām*, a Turkish bath).
‡ *Cossæ* (Khassa) is a muslin of fine texture.
§ Malmul is a variety muslin.
‖ MS. Letter-Books, VII.
** Tafsilah (a cloth from Mecca), *Ain-i-Akbari.*
†† A kind of coarse cotton cloth.

great as it afterwards became. Yet Dacca alone had to supply 85,000 pieces of cotton goods, of which cossæs came to 13,000 and malmuls 15,000.

For the next year the quantities of goods demanded from Madras and Surat showed a gradual decrease, owing perhaps to the vast stocks remaining unsold. But the " Bay " goods (i.e., from the Bay of Bengal) reieceived greater attention and the figures from Bengal went up in most cases. It is likely that this was due to the demand for goods of higher qualities like muslins, which became fashionable among the respectable classes. Madras and Surat goods were chiefly meant for ordinary wear, and the lists of these showed a reduction every year. None of the items entirely disappear ; but there was a diminution in the quantities demanded. In 1683 the longcloths asked for from Madras were 232,000 pieces only. In 1684 the quantity dwindled to 100,000 pieces, and barely 49,000 pieces in 1685. This was true of other varieties also, and some do not make their appearance at all in the list. By 1685 even Bengal goods were asked for in lesser quantities. Dacca had to supply only 3,000 cossæs that year instead of 13,000 in 1682 and 1683. The figures from Surat were also very low : 116,000 bafts, 20,000 chintzes, 16,000 nicarees, no pautkas, 30,000 dungarees. This marked a great fall from the 1682 figures. The reduction in demand during the middle of the decade was such that the Directors even cancelled earlier orders, especially during 1685. The first orders for 10,000 long-cloths, 10,000 percollaes and 31,000 Betelles were replaced by a laconic message, " Send none except 5,000 of the long-cloths."*

This falling off of trade may be accounted for in many ways. First, in those days such commodities as Muslins and Chintzes were wanted only by a few, and even they needed only small quantities. If to-day we do not mark such phenomena, it is because there is an immense variety of stuffs to suit rapidly changing fashions. Secondly, about this time, according to *England's Almanac*, black crape put a check on the use of East India goods. The arrét of

* L.B., VIII, January, 1684.

the French King (1686) prohibiting East Indian calicoes must have also contributed to the dwindling of the Company's business. Although there was a French India Company at the time, the English Company had something like a staple for calicoes on the Atlantic coast of Europe.

However, the turn of the tide soon came. There were signs of a distinct revival of trade towards the late 'eighties.* On August 27, 1688, the Directors wrote " Calicoes of all sorts are in great demand." In 1687, only 13,500 long-cloths were ordered from Madras, but in the next year the figures mounted up to 75,000. The demand in Sallampores was for 41,500 for 1687, and 132,000 for 1688. ' Bay ' goods, too, were wanted in greater quantities. Orders for malmuls stood at 16,500 during both these years. Surat goods still lagged behind. Bafts did not rise above 77,000, which is only a fifth of the 1682 figures. Similarly with chintzes, tapseils, nicarees and other items. Plain calicoes from Bombay were, however, in great demand. The Directors' instruction,† " Bafts are the best commodities you can send us " show in what direction demand was shifting. The use of Indian goods was filtering down to the lower layers of society ; they came to be used " from ladyes down to cook-maids." The Company found this the oppor-tunity for extending its investments.

It was when trade again began to flourish that the " Glorious Revolution " took place in England. Though they lost their greatest patron thereby, the Directors speak in favourable terms of the Prince of Orange in their despatches. " The Prince's army," they wrote, ‡ " do behave themselves civilly paying for their quarters and doing no injury to the country." Interesting details are also found in these letters of the Convention Parliament and other important events of the time.

Nor did the Company suffer by the change of dynasty or by the triumph of the Whigs. Their trade increased rapidly after 1689. Their orders became more frequent and the

* L.B., VIII, August.
† L.B., VIII, March, 1687.
‡ Letter, Vol. IX, p. 1.

investments in India became greater. One reason for this increasing prosperity of the Company was the prohibition of French goods a second time in 1688. The Turkey trade dwindled owing to the war, and this also favoured the Company. Sir Josia Child, then the head of the Company, realised the importance of the situation. " It is good to strike while the iron is hot " wrote this astute diplomat.*
In 1691, the Directors wrote : " You can send us nothing amiss at this time when everything of India is so much wanted."†

The figures in the Despatches mounted up again. In 1690, Madras was asked to supply 160,000 longcloths, 66,000 sallampores and 265,000 neckcloths ; these are nearer the record for 1682 than any intervening years. Bay goods, too, rose in demand. The orders for 1620 were for 40,000 nillæs, 20,000 ginghams, 10,000 malmuls and 10,000 tanjebs. Surat goods rose to such high figures as 180,000 bafts, 77,000 chintzes, 66,000 dungarees and 26,000 tapseils.

This prosperity of the Indian trade did not continue uniformly throughout the decade. About 1695 there was again a fall in demand, owing chiefly to the rising agitation against the trade, and probably also to the war that was then raging. But after 1697 there was renewed prosperity and the figures mounted up again. In 1698 Madras had to supply 150,000 pieces of longcloth, 105,000 ginghams, and 35,000 sallampores.‡ Investments in India increased enormously. In the meantime a new Company had been started to carry on trade with India and there arose keen rivalry between the two Companies. Both tried hard to monopolise the calico trade, and sent out to India vast quantities of bullion for this purpose.

During this period Indian cotton goods were being imported also to Scotland and Ireland and the British Colonies across the seas. The exact figures are not available, but we know that the quantities imported into the American

---

* Raulinson MSS., A 303 (Bodleian).
† Letter books, IX, Jan. 18.
‡ Letter Books, IX, p. 106. " Chintz and all painted stuff turn to good account."

Colonies were considerable. A great deal was sent from England through the legitimate channel ; but the great bulk used in the Colonies were conveyed by illicit traders. The East India Company had the monopoly in these goods even in the Colonies, but the New Englanders had little respect for its monopoly and boldly fitted out piratical expeditions into the East Indies.* They brought vast amounts of calicoes, chintzes, and pepper, and sold them at enormous profit. In 1714, prohibited goods to the value of £10,523 were imported into the American colonies, but this must have been only a fraction of the total imports. There is ample evidence to show that this clandestine trade continued throughout the eighteenth century.

V

Alarming Growth of Calico Fashions

The frequent changings and shiftings of fashion during the period under review can be traced in detail through the despatches of the Directors to the Indian "factories." From 1680 detailed and minute directions were sent to India. "Novel chintzes and calicoes"† were repeatedly called for, because such things proved highly profitable, as they were in great demand among fashionable people. From 1684, Dacca muslins became increasingly popular, and investments in them were multiplied. In 1685, they wrote for Betellees striped with small stripes, for such goods brought by the interlopers fetched fabulous prices. In 1687, striped chintz was more in demand than flowered ones. In the same year, "nillæs with narrow stripes" were much esteemed and so were all goods of lively colours. Neck-cloths were to have a variety of flowers, with a handsome string at the end. Chintzes were becoming most fashionable in high society.‡ In 1688, Sind chintzes were much in demand

---

* Interesting accounts of these are found in the *Documents Relating to the Colonial History of New York*, IV, pp. 300-450, and in Weeden, *Economic and Social History of New England*, 1600-1787.
† Letter Books, VII, July 5, 1682.
‡ Letter Books, VIII, p. 272.

for the higher classes, and the Company knew by experience that it was from those goods that they could gain substantial profits. Hence the repeated orders for finer goods and for various novel designs.

Yet the Company did not neglect the lower classes, because it knew that it was the extended use of any commodity that ultimately gave more profits than the fancy sales of a few choice goods. Like good business men they tried to introduce ordinary fabrics at low prices so that these might ultimately become popular and thereby enlarge their business. In the 'eighties the Company imported vast quantities of cheap calicoes with this object in view, and they were very successful. In 1690, the Directors wrote about plain calicoes that their cheapness had "introduced the wearing the calico in shifts." They ask for sailcloth shifts and longcloth shifts "to be strongly and substantially sewed for poor people's wear."* The Company's attempts at popularising calicoes among the ordinary people seem to have met with great success.

In the nineties, too, similar shiftings of fashion took place. The directors wrote to Bengal for malmuls with great flowers, small stars, birds, beasts, and any other odd fancies of the country.† In another despatch we find : "thin shallow muslins of the slight sorts we were glutted with about three years, have grown into fashion again." After the prohibition the Company counted chiefly upon the finer stuffs, as the duties were equal on all kinds.

It was universally recognised that the general use of calico was harmful to Europe as a whole, that "India and China trade with Europe infinitely to its loss and to their own gain."‡ Of course the chief reason pointed out was the drain of bullion to India, which is complained of in most writings of the period.§ Even Davenant admits that it was an evil. "If all Europe, by common consent," he says, "would agree to have no further dealings to those parts,

---

* Letter Books, VIII, p. 570.
† Letter Books, X, Jan. 26, 1678.
‡ *Advantages of Peace and Commerce*, p. 17.
§ *Essay upon East India Trade*, p. 11.

this side of the world by such a resolution would certainly save a great and continual expence of treasure. For Europe draws from thence nothing of solid use . . . and sends thither gold and silver."* Davenant could find only one point to justify the East India trade, viz., that England could take advantage of Europe's folly. " Since Europe has tasted this luxury and would not give it up," he writes, " let us carry these goods to Europe and gain by the traffic."

Amusing stories were circulated about the havoc worked by these hated Indian goods. *England's Almanac* (1700) narrates how " Lord Godolphin's and Duke of Queensbury's sisters were burnt to death by muslin head-dresses and night-rails ; the Lady Frederick's child burnt to death by Callicoe frock ; a house belonging to St. Paul's School burnt by a Calico bed and curtains, a playhouse at Copenhagen with 3 or 400 people burnt in it occasion'd by callico hangings," and so forth. These instances were meant to remind all persons of the dangerous consequences of the use of calico.

Even more ominous forebodings were made by another writer, who in a quaint pamphlet† entitled " England to be wall'd with gold and to have silver as plentiful as stones in the street, written for the good of the publick, by Joseph Coles,"pronounced his pontifical anathema, in right Biblical language. " O Jerusalem, Jerusalem, thy destruction is of thyself. . . . O, England, strangers devour thee, strangers eat thee up. Thou art fond of novelties which will be thy ruin." He goes on prophesying the decay of his country by its loving other nations too much. Such violent forecasts of imminent danger were bound to have their effect on popular feelings sooner or later.

---

* Brit. Mus., 816 M. 11, No. 92.
† Brit. Mus. 816. m. 12. No. 15.

CHAPTER III

THE DISCONTENT OF ENGLISH INDUSTRIES

I

English Woollen and Silk Industries

BY the seventeenth century the woollen industry had become the backbone of English economic life. Thanks to the influx of foreign skill in the successive migrations of the Flemings in the fourteenth century, the Walloons and Dutchmen in the sixteenth century, and to the active protection which the industry enjoyed under a succession of patriotic kings, England became the leading wool-manufacturing country in Europe, so much so that the jealousy of ambitious foreign kings like Louis XIV was directed against this ' nation of shopkeepers '. When the Old Drapery with its homely broadcloths became old-fashioned, in came the New Drapery under foreign influence with its bays and says its bombazines and moccadoes, and other finer fabrics to suit the taste of the modern Englishmen and Englishwomen who were then being formed under the new influences brought to bear upon social life in the sixteenth and seventeenth centuries. These new industries flourished in Norwich, Colchester, Canterbury, London, and other centres ; and enabled England to " clothe half Europe " and to send her textiles to the uttermost parts of the earth.

The importance of wool and the industries connected with it was a subject on which there had been a wonderful unanimity of opinion among all classes and parties in England. Many patriotic writers went into poetic ecstasy on the subject and indulged in fanciful analogies and allusions. It is one such enthusiast who wrote,* " whether

---

* J. B. *Interest of England considered*, 1717.

THE DISCONTENT OF ENGLISH INDUSTRIES

Ovid alluded to this commodity of ours when Jason sailed to steal the golden fleece assisted by Medea's charms . . . I am not antiquary enough to determine." This was perhaps suggested by the well-known lines of Dryden :

> " Though Jason's fleece was famed of old
> The British wool is growing gold."

The same writer compared wool to Samson's locks, and prophesied evil to it when its destiny should lie in the hands of frivolous women. According to a more serious writer,* Daniel Defoe, English broadcloth was the one unrivalled article of dress suited for every race and climate. He says : " Be their country hot or cold, torrid or frigid, near the Equinox or near the Pole, the English manufacture clothes them all. Here it covers them warm from the freezing of the North Bear ; and there it shades them and keeps them cool from the scorching beams of a perpendicular sun." Even those whose interest happened to lie against the woollen industry have proclaimed the primacy of wool over all other interests. Sir Josia Child, the great champion of the East India trade, declared that wool was " the foundation of English riches." Charles Davenant, next only to Child as protagonist of the same trade, wrote in 1697 ; " As bread is the staff of life, so the woollen manufacture is truly the principal nourishment of our body politic."†

It was this general recognition that the woollen was the staple manufacture in the kingdom that enabled those engaged in it (in Adam Smith's words) " to have been more successful than any other class of workmen in persuad'ng the legislature that the prosperity of the nation depends upon the success and extension of their particular business." No wonder that a fair proportion of the laws entered in the English Statute Book concerns wool. The number of pamphlets written on the subject in the seventeenth and eighteenth centuries is indeed amazing. Government was always expected to protect its interests in a special manner, and its policy, both

---

* *A Plan of English Commerce* (1728).
† *An Essay on East India Trade*, p. 88.

domestic and foreign, was greatly influenced by the woollen interest. It was an unquestioned principle in those countries that England should be up against any trade or commodity that harmed wool in the slightest degree. Such was the situation Indian textiles had to face when they were introduced into England.

Next to wool came silk, which though " a manufacture of foreign extraction," became soon acclimatised in England and " came to a state of great perfection " by the immigration of French artisans in the late seventeenth century. The Huguenots driven from France by the revocation of the Edict of Nantes were welcomed in England, both for their staunch Protestantism and for their exceptional skill in the textile arts. They settled in Canterbury, Spitafields and other places, which thereby soon became flourishing centres for various valuable commodities like high-class silks, brocades, velvets, hats and so forth. The Royal Lustring Company was started in 1692 by some of these immigrants, and this soon obtained a virtual monopoly in many kinds of stuffs. English silks became so famous that as early as 1730 Italian tradesmen had no better device for commending their stuffs than by protesting that those were " right English." The industry grew strong and seems to have absorbed some of those peasants and yeomen evicted by the enclosing landowners. In Spitalfields alone there were about 100,000 weavers towards the close of the seventeenth century. It is said that in 1681 there were in England as many employed in the silk as in the woollen industry.

Such was the position of the leading English industries when the Indian goods arrived in England. But all on a sudden the situation changed for the worse. A contemporary pamphlet summarises it : " Now come our East India gentlemen. . . . The result is that weavers break, journeymen run away having no trade. Some fled to Holland, some to Ireland, some starved to death at home with their wives and children."†

* *Social England* IV, 127.
† *England's Danger by Indian Manufactures* (1699)

THE DISCONTENT OF ENGLISH INDUSTRIES

II

Industrial Crisis

During the last decade of the seventeenth century, the English woollen and silk industries underwent a great crisis. There was unemployment everywhere and the working classes were thrown into a state of intense misery. Frequent representations were made to Parliament, and the petitions received from industrial districts, as we shall see, are full of details of starvation among the labourers. The pamphlets of the period also tell the same tale. No doubt, those Grub-street writers must have exaggerated the case a great deal ; but that there was widespread unemployment and intense misery cannot be questioned. It is well attested by the admissions of Child, Davenant and other supporters of the East India Company.

What was the cause of this misery ? The weavers and the country generally attributed it to the Indian trade. Nor did the Company's protagonists deny it. Child wrote : "I do admit that the wearing of so many printed calicoes had been a prejudice to the complainants and do wish a means might be found to prevent it." Elsewhere, however, he minimises the suffering and even justifies it on the ground that if these were losers by the trade there were others—and in greater number—who gained by it. Of course it was in vain to urge this argument against the premier industry of the time.

The comparative cheapness of calico was at the bottom of these troubles. Consumers at all times and in all countries will buy in the cheapest market, and patriotic considerations are not strong enough to make any drastic change. Indian calicoes and silks enabled people to clothe themselves at a third and (sometimes even a sixth) of the expense normally incurred by the wearers of English woollens and silks. And as for elegance, these foreign goods were superior. Of course, light Indian fabrics and stuffs could not even in summer entirely supply the needs of clothing in England, and so there was a limit to its increased consumption. But it was to the interest of all ordinary people to substitute it for costly English woollens and silks so far as possible, and this was naturally done. Hence the troubles that arose in the latter part of the century.

The importation and use of Indian goods in England not only disorganised the home industries but dislocated foreign trade, and this made the condition at home even worse. The Turkey Company imported silk and silk goods from the Levant in exchange for English woollen exports. When the East India Company brought in cheaper silk from Persia and India, the Levant goods were no longer needed ; and the English merchants who managed the trade, as also the manufacturers who supplied woollen cloth for exportation lost their business. This aggravated unemployment and discontent in the country and made the Turkey merchants the sworn enemies of the East India Company.

England's trade with Central Europe also suffered by the influx of Indian goods. Previously English manufacturers used to send large quantities of woollen cloth to Germany and adjacent countries, but this was in exchange for their linen which was used in England. But when calico displaced German linen, English woollens were no more demanded in Germany and the English weavers as well as traders lost their business. "When we flighted their manufactures they fell on ours."[*] According to Cary, the Germans in retaliation used their linen weaving looms for making woollen cloth and thereby not only dispensed with English goods at home but sent their goods to Poland and other countries. The same happened in respect to other branches of foreign trade.

Calico came to be increasingly used in most European countries, and this indirectly told upon English industries which previously sent cloth to those countries. It has already been shown that the English East India Company itself had been sending large quantities of their goods to America, Spain, and the various English colonies.

Considering all these facts, it was quite natural that the manufacturers put the whole blame upon calico, and calico-importers were hated as the enemies of national prosperity.

* Cary, *Discourse Concerning E. I. Trade* (1698). p. 4.

THE DISCONTENT OF ENGLISH INDUSTRIES

It is now difficult for us to conceive how the Indian imports could have caused such wholesale unemployment. But we must remember that the market for English woollens and silks was in those days very limited. We must also remember that except among the upper classes demand for cloth in those days was very limited, even in England, where the great majority of people have always been better clad than in other countries. It is the variety of clothing and the frequent change of fashions that make demand extensive in these days, but this was hardly the case in Stuart times.

III

The Sufferings of the Industrial Classes

We will now survey the condition of those who were affected by the industrial crisis noted above.

The chief silk manufacturing centres were Spitalfields (Middlesex) and Canterbury. Spitalfields flourished by its popular silks and crapes and brought about a partial revival of English industry after the first triumph of Indian Goods about 1680. According to one writer the stuffs made there by the French settlers " rendered Indian goods contemptible to all sorts of people." As a result of this, " many fields (about the place) were turned into streets, and houses let before they could be finished."* But again Indian goods became popular, and English silks were not wanted, and there followed all the evils of acute unemployment. " Masters who formerly employed twenty or thirty or more cannot now employ four, nor find them full work. The rest are put to miserable shifts and many die of a disease, in plain English, starvation."† Numerous places went under great suffering : Bishopsgate, Aldgate, Cripplegate, Shoreditch, Stepney, Southwark, and the Tower Hamlets. The accounts of the sufferings are heartrending. The thickly-populated bye-lanes and alleys of Bishopsgate " doth

* *England's Advocate* (1699), p. 5.
† *Ibid.*

abound in poverty, the poor rates are doubled."* At Bethnal Green (Stepney) " several of the inhabitants have been reduced to such extremities as to eat horseflesh and grains to support nature."†

Canterbury fared no better. Its silk weaving was started in the reign of Queen Elizabeth and was for long in a flourishing state. But when its goods were no more wanted, the weavers and their employees suffered terribly. According to one account,‡ looms were reduced from one thousand to fifty ; the workers fled to London and Norwich for bread.§ The same was the case with the silk weavers at Norwich, Newbury, Bristol and other centres. Thus " thousands of broad looms and hundreds of throwsters and twisters' mills stand to spoil and ruin."

The way in which the Indian goods drove off English silks is clearly explained by some writers. " When our London and Canterbury weavers, against the spring tide have provided many lutestrings, etc., good as the world can afford, in comes the East India ship with Damasks and Satins which makes the mode for that spring. . . . The ladies are so charmed with it that no other Form or Manner must be the standard of our Mode and Fashion." The weavers somehow sell their goods at a loss and at great expense make the sort of stuffs then in demand. " In comes more East India ships with goods of quite another form ; and all the weavers are in the dirt again."‖ Thus the poor weavers were tired out and some left off the business and took to worsted weaving. This naturally displeased the worsted weavers, who were afraid that their wages would go down.

Nor were the woollen and worsted manufacturers exempt from these troubles. Conditions were especially miserable in Norfolk and Suffolk, and in Gloucestershire. The

* *An English Winding Sheet for Indian Manufactures*, p. 6.
† Hist. MSS. Comm., New Series, Vol. II, 509 (House of Lords MSS.).
‡ " Reflections," p. 6.
§ *England's Danger by Indian Manufactures*, p. 4.
‖ *England's Advocate*, p. 17. As another writer puts it : " when the East India ships come in, half our weavers play." (Quoted in Foster, *East India House*, p. 69.)

Tammete and Green-Say trades of East Anglia were ruined by the use of Indian goods. In Norwich, the then metropolis of the woollen industry, " it was a melancholy sight to see men leave wives and children to parishes, spacious and large trading houses standing empty, . . . landlords abating twenty per cent. of their rents, nay, offering large good houses to any that would keep them in repair."* At Coventry hundreds of workers were out of employment, and the city was described as in a deplorable condition. Many towns and villages in Suffolk, e.g., Sudbury, Coxell, Lavenham, Nailand, Stooke, Needam, Stowmarket—were greatly affected. Even worse was the state of Gloucestershire. It was engaged in making white coarse woollen cloths, which used to be sent to Turkey in return for silk and gogrin yarn for English weavers. But when Turkey silk was driven out by East India commodities about 1678, their cloths would not be bought in Turkey. By 1686, the condition of Gloucestershire became pitiable. Sales declined by about 75 per cent.† This was chiefly due to the disorganisation of their trade with Germany. Poor rates became heavy, and by the end of the century, half the working men of the weaving trade were " running up and down the nation seeking bread from Canterbury to London, from London to Norwich." Their families were left to the parishes for support.

There were many minor trades depending on woollen and silk industries, and these also suffered. The ribbon makers were alarmed, because ribbons were imported under cover of wrought silks, and one such parcel was seized by the Customs House officials. " Their cake is dough," wrote the author of the *English Winding Sheet for East India Manufactures*. Fan-makers, embroiderers and mercers were also affected. What frightened the mercers was the rumour that retail warehouses would soon be opened for East India goods.

The whole country had various vague fears. The rising poor rates of many places alarmed all those whom it affected. The condition of Bethnal Green, as described in a petition‡

* *England's Danger by Indian Manufactures*, p. 2.
† State Papers Domestic, James II, V. 120, 121, etc.
‡ H. MSS. Comm. New Series, Vol. II, p. 509.

to Parliament, was typical of many places. From that petition, signed by the churchwardens, overseers of the poor, and 'ancient' inhabitants of that hamlet, we find that the poor had grown "extremely numerous," that many of the weavers having had no work joined the land and sea forces, "leaving their wives and families a great charge upon the parishes." Some of the weavers who formerly paid the taxes and were themselves forced to receive relief ; and the same happened even to some who had been officers before. The rates and taxes rose suddenly. In Bishopsgate the rates were doubled and the parish became indebted to the amount of £300 on account of poor relief.* In some of the parishes in Gloucester, one-fifth of the whole annual value of land was distributed to the starving poor.†

The landed gentry were greatly alarmed. They feared that their rents would go down. Already this had happened in Norwich and in Spitalfields, and the like fate threatened other places too. Pamphleteers and other agitators put the case in such a way as to alarm the landowners in whose hands lay the strings of power in those days. That remarkable sheet calendar of 1700, *England's Almanac*, put it effectively :

> " Whilst they promote what Indians make
> The employ they from the English take
> Then how shall tenants pay their rent
> When trade and coin to India sent ?
> How shall folks live and taxes pay
> When poor want work and go away ? "

The pamphleteers, by a wild appeal to imagination, tried to show that the whole nation would lose by the disorganisation of the woollen and silk industries. They roused the public by speaking of such consequences as the abatement of the price of land and wool, the fall of rent, the rise of rates and taxes, the loss of revenue, and the depopulation of town and country alike. One writer gave expression to this prophetic warning :‡ " In the end it must produce

---

* *English Winding Sheet for Indian Manufactures*, p. 6.
† Scott, *Joint Stock Companies*, I, p. 309.
‡ *Ibid.*, p. 7

(except to the patentees)* empty houses, empty purses, empty towns, a small, poor, weak and slender people, and what can we imagine the value of our land ? "

IV

How the Weavers won over the Gentry

" The loom, the comb and the spinning wheel
Do all support the nation's weal.
If you'll wear your own silks and woollens
You'll keep your coin, your men, your bullion."
England's Almanac (1700).

The appeal of the weavers to the gentry was a politic move, and there is no doubt that it ensured the success of their cause. A brief analysis of certain socio-economic features of the time will make this clear.

By the Glorious Revolution of 1689, Parliament became sovereign, but Parliament at that time was dominated by the powerful landed gentry of England. Various measures were passed after 1660 to strengthen the power and influence of this class. Feudal tenures were commuted for excise in 1660, and the Corn-bounty Acts of 1673 and 1689 were meant to encourage agriculture and enhance rents.

It is true that there was rising at that time an opulent class of merchants. They, however, did not form a separate class by themselves, but gradually merged into the gentry and became one with them. The successful trader as well as the substantial yeoman was " genteelised " by marriage and ownership of land.† The wealthy 'Nabob' often succeeded not only to the property of the decayed manor but also inherited its local position and influence. This tendency was helped also by the enclosure movement and the dissolution of the monasteries. Nor was this to the detriment of the older gentry in as much as it " supplied the decays " of their ranks. Dr. Johnson might slight this " new species

* *i.e.*, the East India Company.
† See Toynbee, *The Industrial Revolution*, p. 62.

of gentleman " as an intruder ; but no less patriotic an Englishman (Daniel Defoe) averred that the new class was " for gallantry of spirits and greatness of soul, not inferior to the descendants of the best families."

Yet the new trading and industrial classes had yet little influence in Parliament. The landed gentry kept their power for long, and wielded it as it suited their ideas and interests. But the interests of merchants were not altogether neglected. The Navigation Acts of 1651 and 1660, though hurled against Holland, were meant for the merchant's good. Similarly numerous laws were made to prevent the exportation of raw wool in the interests of the manufacturing classes. Apparently this went against the interests of the landowners, because in the absence of a foreign market, English wool was bound to fall in price. How was it that the gentry were prevailed upon to make such a self-denying ordinance ? Adam Smith thought that the simple country gentlemen " were imposed upon by the clamours and sophistry of merchants and manufacturers."* But this view is rather exaggerated. No doubt the pamphleteers on the side of weavers generally overrated the possible injury to land if industry suffered, but there was some truth at the bottom of that argument. The fact is that the landowners honestly believed that they had the same interests as the artisans. If some foreign country imported English wool and set up a competing manufacture, this would ultimately weaken England and the landlords' rents would suffer as much as the profits of the trader and the industrial people. The foreigner would thus reap the benefit. It was this recognition of community of interest that made the gentry enthusiastic about the adoption of measures which apparently benefited the other classes more. No doubt the "gentlemen " were often won to such an attitude by fallacious

* By the term " manufacturer," Adam Smith and other early writers seem to have meant the artisans who worked with the hand. Before the Industrial Revolution, there was no regular class of manufacturers in the modern sense (Hammond, *Town Labourer*, p. 7 ; Toynbee, *Industrial Revolution*, *passim*). The rich clothiers of the time were rather merchants than manufacturers. In the calico-printing industry, however, there seem to have been a few capitalist manufacturers of the modern type. *Infra*, chapter VI, section ii.

arguments, but what influenced their policy most was the widely accepted assumption that whatever affected a part of the body politic would ultimately affect the whole body politic.

However, in the case of the struggle against Indian manufactures, there was not only an apparent identity of interest but a real and substantial one between the gentry and the artisans. The increased use of calicoes and muslins displaced woollen goods not only in England but in the continental markets of England. Thereby English woollens lost the old markets, and necessarily English wool fell. Consequently rents came down ; in some places rents fell so low that they were insufficient even for repairs and taxes.* This by itself was enough to alarm the gentry. Add to this the increased poor rates and other burdens that fell on their depleted purses. Even apart from material considerations, were not the " gentlemen " human enough to sympathise with the miserable weavers and their unemployed workmen ?

The gentry in England have always been interested in the welfare of the manufacturing and trading classes. The younger sons of the gentry were often provided for by being apprenticed to opulent merchants and master craftsmen. It was thus that during the Calico Bill agitation in 1696, a petition was sent to Parliament signed by 281 " gentlemen's sons, apprentices of linen drapers whose guardians had lent considerable sums to the masters." In some cases these genteel apprentices married into the families of their tradesmen employers. These factors tightened the bond between the two classes and made for a solidarity of interests in the country. This had great economic as well as political consequences.

The identity of interests between the various classes has been well brought out by the vigorous mercantilist writer, John Cary. He says :† " The freeholder raises the

---

* See Scott, *Joint Stock Companies*, II, p. 136.
† *An Answer to Some of the Linnen Drapers' Objections* (1696?), p. 2. (British Museum, 816. m. 13. No. 140.)

product, while the trader* manufactures and exports it to the foreign markets ; the former furnishes provisions whilst the others are employed in commerce and by mutual harmony both live happily." These two interests, he maintained, must be harmonised if the country should prosper. He also ingeniously argued that the consequences of a clash of interests would be more serious to the landowners. " Once if these two interests jar with each other and such a freedom granted to the trader, that he should cease to depend on the freeholder, and the freeholder to be encouraged by him, the lands of England must fall." Indeed, this argument easily appealed to the gentry.

The merchants always took pains to show that the gentry gained most by the alliance. And they argued it in such a plausible way that few questioned its soundness at the time. Cary was again the best exponent of this view. " A free liberty to import corn would supply it cheaper from outside than the rents of England can afford ; should a free liberty be given to export wool and to import the manufactures made thereof, 'twould be all one to the trader, whose profits would arise from both ; but whether this freedom of commerce would be in the interest of the freeholder, and consequently to the interest of England, I leave to an impartial judge. Nothing advances the lands of England like the manufactures, which makes the products valuable."†

In the above passage, however, Cary tries to view the 'manufacturers' and the traders as belonging to one class. But it is evident that their interests were not quite identical. It did not perhaps matter to the trader whether English wool was worked up at home or sent out of the country ; but to the manufacturer it constituted his bread and butter. This was the reason why the gentry were more attached to the 'manufacturers' than to the traders; and in the calico controversy of 1696-1700, this can be seen clearly enough. Foreign manufactures worked havoc on home industries and also

---

* Here Cary used the word " trader " to mean both merchants and craftsmen, but in the passage quoted in the next paragraph he apparently uses it to mean only the former.

† *Ibid.*, p. 3.

affected the landlord's rents ; but it afforded profitable trade to the merchant, and only those merchants who, like the interlopers, wanted to break the Company or, who, like the Turkey traders, exported woollen cloth, were interested in prohibiting calico imports. The gentry as a whole were therefore for protective legislation as much in their own interests as in those of the weavers, and this ensured the success of the agitation for prohibiting Indian manufactured goods.

V

Early Legislation against Indian Import Trade

In spite of the combination of interests of the various classes in England as noted above, it was not very easy to convince Parliament that protective legislation against the Indian textile trade was necessary. As early as 1675 the matter came before Parliament, but no successful legislation was effected for quarter of a century.

The agitation against Indian silks and calicoes began almost simultaneously with the growth of import trade in them. According to *England's Almanac*, 1674 was the fatal year when printed calicoes superseded the use of green says, " Tammits," and other English stuffs. And about the same time, the first petition against Indian textiles was laid before Parliament by some clothiers of Gloucestershire and Worcestershire. According to Child,* this was drawn up by malicious individuals who had some private grudge against the Company, or who were bribed to do so by the Turkey merchants or the foreign enemies of the English Company. And he slyly adds : " Whether they were Dutch or English that paid the best fees, that I could never discover." He admits that there was a real grievance for the clothiers of Kent and Suffolk who lost much of their trade, but they had not complained. The actual petitioners " do now make and vend above twenty times the quantity of cloth which they did before the Company was erected."

* *The East India Trade most National* (1681), pp. 19-20.

Nothing came immediately out of this petition. Those were days when the Company enjoyed the patronage of a king who, in spite of his faults, was intensely popular with his subjects. Besides, Parliament was prorogued till 1677. The matter was, however, taken up by Parliament in connection with an allied trade question, and the Whig party, just coming into being, took up the cause of the English weavers. In February, 1677, there was an acrimonious discussion in the House of Commons on a Bill for preventing the exportation of wool, in which several prominent persons like Thomas Papillon and Colonel Birch took part. The latter has gained Macaulay's praise for his " strong sense and mother wit " and " great talents for business." He introduced the question of Calicoes into the discussion ; but unfortunately we get only faint echoes of the parliamentary debates of those days. " One commodity more ruins us," he said, " and that is calico, which destroys more the use of wool than all things besides. You encourage the trade with heathens who work for a penny a day and destroy Christians ; and the French who scarcely cut flesh four times a year and wear linen breeches and wooden shoes, destroy your trade by underselling you. That of Ireland is but a minute thing in comparison of the rest. You pay £180,000 a year upon account of very kitchen maids who will wear hood and scarves."*

Though the House did not grasp the full force of the question presented by the talented Colonel they gave their enthusiastic consent to a resolution passed in the same year to guard English woollens against the competition of foreign goods. This resolution commanded all persons whatsoever to wear no garment, stockings, or other sort of apparel but what is made of sheep's wool only from the feast of All Saints to the feast of Annunciation of our Lady inclusive."† This was followed by an act that insisted on people being buried in woollen instead of linen.

> " Since the living would not bear it
> They should when dead be forced to wear it."

* Gray's Debates of the House of Commons, Vol. III, p. 430.
† 18 & 19 Ch. II, c. 4.

THE DISCONTENT OF ENGLISH INDUSTRIES

In 1680, the question cropped up again in connection with a petition sent up by the Company of silk-weavers in London. The Parliament of 1680 was veritably " a revolutionary assembly " which witnessed many stormy scenes connected with the Exclusion Bill and other high matters of state, and the question of the East India trade was therefore relegated to a secondary place. Yet we read of a rather heated discussion, in which Birch and Pollexfen took part.* Both of them severely attacked the Company's policy of sending out patterns and artificers to India, and showed how English manufactures had been displaced by Indian goods. From the way in which they spoke, it would appear that they were advocates of the Turkey Company, which was then openly inimical to the sister corporation. This was also the impression gained by John Smith who reviewed the debate in his *Chronicon Rusticum commerciale* (1747)†. The petition was referred to the Grand Committee for Trade, but practically nothing came out of it.

This debate, however, called forth two able pamphlets in defence of the East India Trade, one by Thomas Papillon and the other by Josia Child. Papillon's *A Treatise on East India Trade,*‡ published in 1686, supported the calico trade as it was " a most useful and necessary commodity " and " serving instead of the like quantity of French, Dutch and Flanders Linnen which would cost at least three times the price of it." Child's reply§ was more thorough-going and made a searching analysis of the whole trade. He tried to to show that the trade enriched the nation annually by increasing shipping and volume of trade, and ably maintained that the manufactured goods of India were such as to displace only the imports from Holland and other countries, and thereby brought a gain to the nation of above a million pounds sterling per annum. As for raw silk, he admitted that the cheaper and better silks of India " probably touch

* India Office Tracts 53 A. 11.
† Vol. I, p. 355.
‡ Goldsmiths' Library.
§ " A Treatise . . . . East India Trade the most National " (1681).

63

some Turkey merchants' profit at present "; but he maintained that this was a profit to the Kingdom in as much as it would reduce the cost of manufactures. He knocked the bottom out of the Turkey merchants' complaint when he wrote : "What then ? must one trade be interrupted because it works upon another ? At that rate there would be nothing but confusion *ad infinitum.*"*

Yet it was not the cogency of these arguments, so far as we know, that disarmed the opposition against the Company, and left it unmolested in the full enjoyment of its trade until the next attack of 1696. It was due chiefly to the timely transformation of the Company into a " Tory corporation " so dramatically described by Macaulay. After the sensational incidents that culminated in the boisterous Oxford Parliament (1681) the Whigs (to whom, by the way, Balliol gave quarters) were completely defeated and the Tories (who supported the King and the Stuart Cause) had a complete triumph. About the same time Whigs like Papillon were thrown out of the governing body of the Company. Child, fawning before the triumphant King, became supreme ; and so long as the Tory cause prospered, no one could do any harm to Sir Josia Child or against the trading Company, of which he was the uncrowned King.

Nor did Sir Josia lack the art of keeping people in good humour. By various methods of cajolery and bribery he kept the favour of the Court. William Love in 1680 explained to Parliament some of these arts : " New year's gifts . . . getting others into the company and choosing them of the Committee, though they understood no more of trade than I of physic ; also naming ships by great men's names" and so forth. " Prince Butler "† has given a graphic description of the " craft of the great Goliah," who gave

> ". . . great gifts of finest touches
> To lords and ladyes, Dukes and Duchess."

It was perhaps thus that Child stopped further proceedings in the Committee for Trade on the petition of 1680,

* *op. cit.*, p. 12.
† Prince Butler's Case, representing the wool case (Bodl. θ658).

and the following passage most probably refers to that transaction :

> " The case thus heard, they were inclined
> Some proper remedy to find. . . .
> But by the craft of great Goliah
> Who all the world stood defy-a
> There is this story passing current
> That say it was he stopped the torrent
> By pouring gold in plenteous showers,
> In ladyes' laps that bore great powers,
> Which strangely altered all their measures
> Such charms there are in hidden treasures."

That the Company in those days resorted to such discreditable means is evident from the inquiries instituted by the House of Commons in 1695.* In the account books of the Company were found large sums—as high as £11,372 for 1691—as having been spent for " secret service." When all these were detected, the clever Sir Josia " screened himself behind his creature and connection by marriage, Sir Thomas Cooke, who was committed to the Tower by the Commons, and bemoaned himself weeping at the Bar of the Lords."

For a time after 1680 the weaving industry was comparatively prosperous. According to *England's Almanac*, " black crape put check upon East India goods and English good still flourished after 1680." The resolution of 1677 and the statute about burying in woollen must also have produced satisfactory results. Besides, a heavy customs duty was imposed upon Indian cloth about that time. This naturally caused a fall in the calico imports of the East India Company and made for the encouragement of English weaving.

The king's customs had been regarded in the past more as a source of revenue than as a means of protecting home industries. But in the hands of Parliament, tariff legislation became predominantly protective. Before 1660,

---

* See also Macaulay, Works III, 473 :—" All who could help or hurt at Court, ministers, mistresses, priests, were kept in good humour by presents of shawls and silks, birds' nests and attar of roses, bulses of diamonds and bags of Guineas."

calicoes paid only the uniform duty of five per cent. ad valorem, but at the Restoration, Parliament allowed Charles II to levy an additional duty—" one full moytie " over and above the previous rate—on all linen imported into England, including therein calicoes and India-wrought silks. The Company denied to the Customs authorities in 1664 that calico was linen, but the latter did not admit the contention.* Every piece of calico henceforward had to pay a duty of from 9d. to 3s. Of course, owing to the low cost price of calicoes, the Company did still make good profits, and the Indian goods being popular in England, the duty hardly served for protective purposes. In 1685, another additional duty of ten per cent. ad valorem was sanctioned by Parliament " on all calicoes and all other Indian linen imported from the East Indies, and all wrought silks or manufactures of India made of or mixed with herba or silk and thread or cotton imported into England from the East." The ostensible object of this imposition was to find funds for James II's campaign against the Duke of Monmouth, but protection was undoubtedly uppermost in the minds of the legislators. Although this duty was granted only until 1690, it was not allowed to cease in that year. It was confirmed and doubled instead, with the object of providing the " means of necessary defence of the realms, the perfect reducing of Ireland and the effectual prosecution of war against France."

These repeated impositions discouraged the use of Indian calicoes and silks to a certain extent, but owing to their comparative cheapness the duties were easily borne, and did not reduce the trade to any appreciable degree. On the contrary, Indian imports were on the increase, and towards the closing years of the century, England was flooded with Indian calicoes and silks.

---

* They had in those days no exact knowledge as to whether calico was linen. Thus Pepys writes in 1664 :—" Sir Martin Noel told me that the dispute between him . . . . and the East India Company is whether calico be linen or no, which he says it is and having ever been returned so. They say it is made of cotton wool and grows upon trees."

CHAPTER IV

PROTECTIONISM *versus* FREE TRADE

I

The Controversy

ALL through the latter half of the seventeenth century the protectionist doctrine was effectively preached by a galaxy of patriotic writers. Indeed it was popular among the classes and even among the masses ; yet it did not immediately shape the economic policy of the State. Charles II was compelled by the nationalist party in Parliament to adopt a protectionist attitude towards foreign trade, but this did not become the confirmed policy of the State until after the Glorious Revolution. In the meantime a vigorous protectionist propaganda was carried on in England in the interests of the woollen and silk manufactures, and the Indian trade which was the ostensible rival of these manufactures became the target of virulent attacks, not only of those engaged in the industries concerned, but of the mercantilist enthusiasts who took up their cause. The result was a series of Parliamentary enactments mainly connected with Indian trade, which made protectionism the sheet anchor of English economic policy for more than a century. This legislation also brought the economic principles involved to the forefront. The theoretical background of protectionism was clearly laid down by a set of talented writers, who appealed not to sordid self-interest but to national solidarity and collective well-being. The vehemence of their exposition naturally produced an opposition equally vehement, which necessarily took the form of what is familiar to us as free trade. For the first time, an appeal was made to free trade as the most rational of trade policies, and although it did not convince contemporaries, those able writers are entitled to our respect for their marvellous anticipations of modern economic doctrines. The last decade of the seventeenth century was thus a " seed-time " in the history of economic thought. At no period before Adam Smith did economic theory make such rapid strides. However, this advance of theory was not the result of any scientific controversy, but was made mainly in connection with a humdrum dispute about the calico trade, in which those who had material interests at stake took active part. The protagonists on neither side were directly interested in the advance of economic science. With hardly any exception, they were not theorists or scholars but practical men arguing out a practical question of material importance to themselves. Yet, although devoid of book-learning, they had acquired practical knowledge from worldly experience and had plenty of shrewd common sense. Nor were they impartial ; they were but partisans advocating a cause to which they were pledged. They wrote party pamphlets, not economic treatises. One should not expect balanced judgment from such writings ; yet their value as economic literature can hardly be questioned. Great credit is due to them for clarifying economic conceptions and for originating much of the theoretical background of the protectionist and free trade views.

The calico controversy of 1696-1700 was fought mainly by means of pamphlets and broadsides. The volume of such publications is marvellous, even judging from those now preserved in the accessible British archives in London and Oxford. No doubt many of the publications were worthless repetitions of stilted arguments,* yet there were writers of outstanding ability on both sides and their pamphlets deserve to be treated as economic literature of a high order. Even the semi-comic *Querical Demonstrations*

---

* According to W. A. S. Hewins, " Men wrote pamphlets, not because after a careful and impartial investigation, they had discovered important principles which it was desirable that the world should know, but to defend the interests of some section whose interests were attacked, to support a project to which subscriptions were invited, or to urge some remedy for evils in the State." (*English Trade and Finance chiefly in the seventeenth century*, p. xvi.)

of " Prince Butler " are not so light as they look on the surface.

John Pollexfen was the foremost among the writers who took up the weavers' cause. One of the Commissioners of Trade and Plantations, Pollexfen was an influential person and his views commanded respect both in Parliament and outside. There is no reason to suppose that his advocacy of protectionism was actuated by any narrow self-interest. He was probably a genuine patriot enamoured of the mercantilist ideal. Pollexfen reminds one more of the high-souled puritan heroes of the Civil War than his time-serving contemporaries. The pamphlets* he published and the papers laid by him before Parliament were the mine from which the party-hacks got their powder and shot. He attacked Davenant's *Discourse of the East India Trade*, and the latter's reply by no means refuted his arguments.

Another serious writer who supported the Protectionist cause was John Cary.† He was one of the ablest exponents of mercantilism. John Locke, the philosopher, read and appreciated the writings of this "worthy man and disinterested lover of his country"‡; and was even "ambitious" of his acquaintance. Nor was he a mere partisan. For, as a consistent mercantilist, he advocated the planting of a calico industry in England—a suggestion that was calculated to displease and even alarm the weavers. Cary had a rather protracted scuffle with the linen-drapers in 1696, and a series of broadsides were issued by both parties. It is interesting to see how his nationalist position was assailed by the free trade challenge of the drapers. To many at the present day, the drapers' argument might appear more

* The best known are (1) *A Discourse of Trade, Coin and Paper Credit* (1697); (2) *England and India Inconsistent in their Manufactures* (1698). Pollexfen is called "one of the company's most influential enemies." (Wisset, *Compendium on East India Affairs* (1800), p. 48.

† He published many Essays on Trade between 1695 and 1700, of which special attention might be directed on his *Discourse Concerning East Indian Trade* (1696); *Discourse of East India Trade a most unProfitable Trade* (1699); and his answers to Linen Drapers contained in Brit. Mus. 816. m. 13.

‡ Locke's letter to Cary, April 12th, 1696. Brit. Mus. MSS. 5540, fol. 68.

sound, but to contemporaries Cary's view must have appealed more effectively.

The great majority of the writers who supported the weavers were of an inferior order. Of them " Prince Butler " was veritably the prince.* He was a humourist and shows great skill in bringing Josia Child to ridicule. He wrote many ballads and satires on the East India trade and they " generally began o'er a pot of ale," as he himself 'admits. His pedantry and alliterations are perhaps nauseating, yet his *Querical Demonstrations* put the weavers' case most emphatically. With effective sarcasm he rebutted the arguments of the Company. " Had not," he asked, " a hundred thousand poor rather come to their Parishes for want of work, and all the land of England fall two years' purchase, than that the Cookmaids should not be cloathed in India silk and the ladies in Callicoes ? "

More serious writers than Butler were " T.S. " and " N.C.," both weavers.† They have given useful facts about the decay of woollen and silk manufactures, and tried to answer Davenant's contention that the Indian trade did not injure these industries. There were many other pamphlets and broadsides published, mostly anonymous, all vying with one another in throwing discredit on the Company. Nor were they all couched in terms of abuse. Some made pathetic appeals to their fellow citizens, and particularly begged the women-folk to leave off wearing calicoes. " Now, ladies," wrote one of them, ‡ " we are in a great danger. If you do deliver us now, women shall wear crowns of gold. The child unborn will bless you," and so forth.

On the opposite side there were abler writers. Child was the brain of the defence until he died in 1699. His *New Discourse of Trade* was published in 1690, just before

---

* His writings are :—(1) *Querical Demonstrations* ; (2) *Prince Butler's Tale* (verse) : and *Queries relating to the East India Trade*. All are in the Bodleian.

† Two of T.S.'s pamphlets are in the Bodleian ; *England's Danger by Foreign Manufactures*, and *Reasons humbly offered for passing a Bill prohibiting Silks*, etc., (1697).

‡ *An Address to the Ladies*. Brit. Mus. 816. m. 12. (No. 15), p. 8.

the struggle thickened; but the same was re-published with additions in 1694. He also wrote other tracts like *The Great Honour and Advantage of East India Trade* (1697) : and the able defence of the Company before Parliament came from his fertile brain. Next to Child, but in some respects above him, stands Dr. Charles Davenant as a protagonist on the Company's side. He was the son of the well-known poet and dramatist, Sir William Davenant, and was educated at Balliol College, Oxford.* Leaving Oxford without a degree, Charles Davenant entered politics as a Tory under James II, and for a long time he was one of the galaxy of writers who supported the Tory party. Macaulay calls him " a most unprincipled and rancorous politician," but we must remember that Macaulay's views were often coloured by his Whig prejudices. The Company employed him for various transactions and in the able defence he put up for his employers, he " stumbled on economic doctrines which seem to foreshadow the conclusions of a later age."† He wrote two able treatises on the East India Trade, *The Essay* in 1697, and *The Discourse* in 1699. The latter work was written to answer Pollexfen's arguments. Davenant was very ably attacked by the weavers, and it is difficult to say that they were refuted by him.

Those were days of brilliant pamphleteering. We can almost conjure up the conditions under which the above warfare went on. Some poor printer of Grub Street brings out a pamphlet, and that very day it forms the chief topic in the crowded coffee-houses of the day. The little politicians wax eloquent over the merits of the case. Perhaps a reply is suggested on the spot to an ingenious " Prince Butler," and he makes capital of it the next day. Somehow, the calico controversy made great commotion in London, at least in 1696 and 1697.

In brief, the weavers' contention was that all their ills were due to the East India trade, and that the Company sent out artificers and patterns to India and thereby taught the

* Dict. Nat. Biogr. Vol. XIV. Sir W. Davenant is supposed to have been a natural son of Shakespeare.
† P. E. Roberts, in *British India*, Vol. II, p. 350.

people there to make stuffs suited to the English market, and that the goods so brought supplanted the use of English manufactures both at home and abroad. Germany and Turkey used to take English woollens in exchange for their linen and raw silk respectively, but when Indian calicoes and silks drove them out, English woollens did not sell any more in those countries; and this resulted in the dislocation of these two trades and the industries that supplied them with cloth. The weavers were also supported by bullionists, who still kept up the cry that India drained the country of its treasure. That they found support with the Government is evident from the preamble to the Prohibition Act of 1700, which recounts the exhaustion of treasure.

The Company based its defence not upon practical demonstration of facts (as did the weavers) but upon certain new theoretical conceptions which were hardly calculated to appeal to, let alone convince, that generation. Its supporters insisted that trade should not be burdened with prohibitions or tariffs. But as there existed a general agreement at that time among all parties in the State that trade should be regulated by Government to suit the interests of the country, the Company's appeal to Free Trade fell upon deaf ears, and its cause was bound to fail for the time being.

We will now proceed to examine the rival positions.

II

Protectionism

The whole contention of the Protectionists was based upon the Nationalist conception of the State as an economic entity. England being an independent nation must have a definite national policy, and all its energies must be directed toward the development of its resources. There were certain national industries which enriched the State and supplied employment to the people. The preservation of these was the prime concern of Government. Foreign trade, especially the import trade with India, harmed these industries. Cheap Indian goods brought from India displaced the dearer English commodities not only in England but in English markets abroad. English industries were thus ruined, and this meant a serious national calamity. The rent of land (which constituted the income of the predominant classes) was also bound to fall in consequence ; and it actually fell in some places. No doubt the consumer was benefited by the cheapness of Indian goods, but the consumer's interest was not the concern of the State. Mercantilists identified the interests of the State with the interests of the producer ; The well-being of the State was bound up with the prosperity of the industrial classes. This was the protectionist position in a nutshell.

Thus the crux of the protectionist contention was that foreign trade must be so regulated as to benefit the national industries of England.* As has been pointed out above, all foreign trade was judged good or bad from this standpoint. Nor did the protectionist writers leave the issues obscure. Great pains were taken by them to define the criteria of a good trade. According to Cary, a trade was advantageous to the kingdom if it (i.) exported from the country home products and manufactures ; (ii.) imported into the country such commodities as may be manufactured there or be used up in home manufactures; (iii.) supplied certain things without which the kingdom cannot carry on its foreign trade, and (iv.) which encouraged navigation and increased seamen. A good trade imported raw produce and exported manufactured commodities, and thus enriched the State by bringing in treasure from other countries and providing employment for the artisans of the country. Any trade that brought in manufactured goods or sent out raw produce was therefore injurious to the State, and must be checked by the State. This was the orthodox mercantilist view on trade policy, and few disagreed with this at the time.

Thus the ideal before the Mercantilists was a wealthy and powerful nation, getting richer every year at the expense of other countries.

The Mercantilists had also vivid notions as to what national prosperity meant. They measured it mainly by

* See Cunningham (Modern Times), p. 459.

73

(i.) a dense population and (ii.) profitable employment for the whole population.   As Clayton puts it, " National happiness consists in a fruitful soil, multitudes of people, and these people fully employed in beneficial trade."* The writers of the the time were vying with one another in devising practicable means " for a most ample increase of the wealth and strength of England in a few years," or " how England could be wall'd with gold and to have silver as plentiful as the stones in the street." They were all honest enthusiasts, the glorious representatives of a patriotic age.

The importance of population was a common topic among all the writers of the period, and there was hardly any economic pamphleteer who neglected this item of national prosperity.   Both mercantilists and their critics agreed on this point.   All of them, however, did not deal with " Political Arithmetick " as did Sir William Petty.† But they always took it for granted that " multitudes of people are the real strength of the nation and the riches of it also."   Even Child admitted that " It is multitudes of people and such laws as cause an increase of people which principally enrich any country."   According to Davenant, " People are the most important strength for any nation." ‡ As for the weavers and their writers, there was nothing which they emphasised more than the need of an abundant population.

This anxiety about population looks to us rather strange at the present time, but perhaps it was justified by the special circumstances of the seventeenth century.   The population of England in that period was much less than that of her rival, France, and it tended to remain stationary for a long time.   In 1688, Gregory King calculated it to be five-and-a-half millions, but in 1750, Finlaison could not find more than six million inhabitants in England.   Economic writers of the time looked upon this state of affairs with serious misgivings, because they were agreed that a large population was necessary to promote the numerous commercial enterprises of England.

* *A Short System of Trade* (1719).
† For Petty's views, see *Treatise on Taxes*, Vol. I, p. 22.
‡ *Discourse on Public Revenues and on the Trade of England.*   Disc. III.

The more plentiful the population, the larger was the trade of the nation, and trade was universally regarded as the means by which treasure flowed into the country. Population was thus looked upon as a factor in production, and it was in relation to this that its importance was emphasised.

It was not enough, however, to have a large population ; it was even more important that they should be fully employed. An unemployed population was regarded as a great drag on prosperity, and not only local bodies but the central Government were actively engaged in creating employment. Laws were frequently passed in Parliament for this purpose : even the Act of 1700 prohibiting calicoes was called the " Bill for effectual employing of the Poor in the Kingdom." Many schemes for supplying employment were from time to time propounded by patriotic writers. This conception of national responsibility for unemployment was a potent factor in the economic policy of the time. It led to many familiar fallacies. Cary, for instance, maintained in defence of the weavers that woollen cloth, however dear, was profitable to England, for he said, " Woollen cloth costs us only labour " ; and adds in explanation : " Our people must be maintained though they be idle."

Such views are due to the exaggerated importance of production as against consumption, and of exportation as against importation. Production was all-important, because it supplied commodities for the foreign market and thereby increased trade and brought treasure into the country.*
The interests of the consumers never entered into the calculations of Mercantilists.

The protectionists thus made out a strong case against the Indian trade. Some of them insisted that the Indian manufactures should be totally prohibited, for otherwise

* " For a hundred years past, the English have considered export-ation, and sale of goods and merchandise abroad, as the only profitable and advantageous trade to the Kingdom, and on the contrary left it very doubtful whether the importation of goods be beneficial or preju-dicial." Quoted by Cunningham (*Growth of English Industry and Commerce* [Modern Times] p. 406), from a Dutch writer of the eighteenth century.

"'like the ill-favoured lean kine, they will destroy the use of our manufactures which might be fitted to answer all the ends they (Indian goods) serve for."* And if such a stringent law was put into effect, "we should not want workhouses for the employment of our poor in the country or city ; nor the Turkey or Italian merchants want vend for their cloths and stuffs abroad or silk at home."† Others, however, were more reasonable. They did not want to prohibit Indian manufactures absolutely, but wished to impose a tariff upon them high enough to eliminate the advantage then enjoyed by Indian cloth in the English market. In their view, such tariffs were to be based on a calculation of the wages and other expenses in the two countries.

The position thus taken up by the mercantilists was accurately stated and logically maintained. They were the first to embody into a coherent system the vague protectionist ideas which were already in the air. Much credit is due to them for the crystallisation of these ideas. Protectionism thus became a *system* with definite principles and advocating a definite policy.

III

The Free Trade View of Child and Davenant

The protectionists firmly laid it down that the Indian trade must be discouraged as it involved the impoverishment of the country. This proposition went right against the self-interest of the East India Company, and of the linen drapers who dealt in Indian cloth. Especially for the Company it was a matter of life and death to defend the Indian trade from the aspersions cast on it. In the face of the hard facts of industrial decay known to every one, it was not possible for the Company's protagonists to deny flatly that the Indian imports harmed English industries. They could maintain, as they did maintain, that although

* Cary, *Discourse*, pp. 3-4.
† *An English Winding Sheet*, p. 7.

the Indian trade was detrimental to certain industries, the general prosperity of the nation was promoted by that trade. Child and Davenant argued this out at length by pointing to the increase of shipping and seamen, influx of treasure, and the general growth of wealth in the country. Child wrote that the Indian trade had " been the greatest engine that has wrought us into that Fund of Wealth, which served not only to enrich us in Peace but has enabled us to defend ourselves thus long at so great expense against the invasion of the most powerful enemy (France) towards which extraordinary service I think it need not be doubted that the East India trade has contributed in proportion, as much if not more than others."*

Such a general defence, however, was not calculated to satisfy any one. A definite charge had been made against the Indian import trade and its evil effect upon national industries had been demonstrated. To this, a direct reply was necessary. Such a reply was not possible without questioning some of the assumptions of mercantilist economics ; and this was what Child, Davenant, and other writers did.

Their main contention was that it was ultimately more advantageous to the kingdom to leave trade free from restraints. They argued that free trade would lead to the expansion of commerce and thereby bring more wealth into the kingdom ; if restraints were put on it trade would dwindle and along with it also the wealth of the country. No doubt the Indian trade injured certain industries, but this was explained away by Davenant by a sensible appeal to an international specialisation in industries, while *The Considerations on East India Trade* even went further and demonstrated that it was loss to the kingdom to carry on manufactures which could be managed elsewhere with the labour of fewer hands and thus more cheaply. This view foreshadowed the modern theory of comparative costs. It is also significant that an appeal was made so early to an

* *The Great Honour and Advantage of the East India Trade to the Kingdom asserted* (1697), p. 45.

international system of economics as opposed to the national system which found favour at that time.*

Before proceeding further it might perhaps be advisable to define the term Free Trade, because, as is well known, that phrase has been used in many different senses in the sixteenth and seventeenth centuries. According to Professor Foxwell there were at least six different uses current during that period. † It may be noted, however, that there is one underlying idea in all those different uses of the term. " Free Trade " invariably meant freedom from restraints on trade. Such restraints were mainly of two kinds : (i.) Exclusive monopoly given to trading companies and (ii.) the imposition of protective tariffs on, or absolute prohibition of imported goods. In the first half of the century the question of monopoly gave an occasion to controversy, and hence the " Free Trade " Bills, and the term " free traders " applied to interlopers. But when high tariffs were put upon foreign imports later on, merchants spoke of freeing trade from such restraints, and thus came into currency the use of the term to mean freedom from protective tariffs and prohibitions. It was in this latter sense that Child and Davenant used the term, and this was followed by the linen drapers and others who took part in the controversy of 1696-1700. ‡ Thus the term Free Trade had attained its present sense by the close of the seventeenth century, but it is not denied that subsequently it has been misused.

The Company's exposition of Free Trade is contained in the writings of Child and Davenant, and in the numerous broadsides published in 1696 and 1699. It was Davenant, however, that supplied the central arguments.

---

* The interdependence of the whole world in the matter of trade has been very well brought-out by a contemporary, Sir Dudley North, in a few pregnant statements :—" The whole world as to Trade is but as one Nation or People, and therein Nations are as Persons." " The loss of Trade with one Nation is not that only separately considered, but so much of the Trade of the world rescinded and lost, for all is combined together." (*Discourses upon Trade*, 1691.)

† See for instance Brit. Mus. 816 m. 13. No 141 ; 143. The quotations given below will clear the point.

‡ In private correspondence.

PROTECTIONISM *versus* FREE TRADE

Both Child and Davenant fought vehemently against restrictions on trade. According to Child, "liberty and property conduce to the increase of trade." All clogs in trade were harmful to the kingdom, and this might be learnt from the experience of the various countries. He also laid it down that it was the interest of England "to go to a cheap market for the goods we stand in need of." Davenant put the view in more sonorous language. He wrote*: " Trade is in its nature free, finds its own channel and best directeth its own course." All laws to give it rules and directions and to limit and circumscribe it may serve the particular ends of private men but are seldom advantageous to the public." He supported a moderate *Laissez Faire* policy. " They say few laws in a state are an indication of wisdom in the people ; but it may be more truly said that few laws relating to trade are the mark of a people that thrives by traffic."† He therefore condemned the law about burying in woollen as foolish and wasteful.

Davenant tried to justify the free trade view by arguments drawn both from theory and practice. He believed in an international division of labour arranged by nature. Each country must specialise in the production of those commodities for which it was naturally fitted! " The various products of different soils and countries " he stated,‡ " is an indication that Providence intended they should be helpful to each other and mutually supply the necessities of one another. Just as it is a great folly to compel a youth to that sort of study to which he is not adapted by genius or inclination so it is unwise to introduce into a country the growth of commodities not suited to its potentialities." The practical point he had to drive home was that England need only look to the interests of the woollen industry (which calico did not harm) and not to those of silk or linen which were exotic trades (and which felt aggrieved at the import of calicoes). England could make woollens cheap and no other country could undersell her

* Works II, p. 98.
† Op. cit. p. 99.
‡ Works I, pp. 104-105.

if she did so. Therefore he pointed out that it was the interest of England to concentrate all her energies on wool and introduce all economies in it rather than work industries which were unsuited to the country. " Our soil and the labour of our people," he said, " can be employed about materials more advantageous and wherein we cannot be undersold by other countries."

This argument, however, was like gall and wormwood to the silk weavers at Spitalfields and Canterbury. They maintained that the silk industry was as much an English manufacture as the woollen and employed almost as many labourers. Against this claim, the Company, the linen drapers, the calico printers and others engaged in the calico trade urged that they were also " a numerous people " and that the prohibition of calicoes would cause misery to large numbers among them.

Here arose the vital question as to whose interest was to prevail among the competing industries. Child wrote : " At this rate the brewers may be opposed to the vintners, the weavers of worsted against silk weavers, Norwich against Spitalfields."*

Davenant used another very ingenious argument which caused much hair-splitting among the rival pamphleteers. He maintained that it was to the interest of England to have woollen cloth manufactured cheap, so that English traders might undersell all other countries. The competition of cheap Indian cloth served this purpose and thereby the use of calico was ultimately a help to the woollen industry. In another way he tried to show that the woollens were benefited by the use of calicoes. He assumed that the profit from woollens arose, not from what were consumed at home but from those sent abroad. " If the people of England are willing and pleased to wear Indian silks and stuffs of which the prime cost in India is not above a fourth part of what their own commodities would stand them in here ; and if they are thereby enabled to export so much of their own products, whatever is so saved is clear gain to the kingdom in general."†

* *The Great Honour and Advantage of the East India Trade* (1697).
† Works II, p. 102.

The weavers were rather amused by this clever sophistry of Davenant, and answered this by taunts and sarcastic hits. Prince Butler took a special delight in exposing the weakness of Davenant's arguments by pushing them to their logical conclusions. " Would it not be better," he asked, " to employ the Dutch ships, for they always sail much cheaper than we do, and then we may send our own ships to foreign nations that want to hire them ? " Cary, however, took the argument more seriously. He denied that Indian calicoes and silks were really cheaper than English manufactures ; for, he said, the latter cost England nothing but labour above the materials whereof they were made, and by using them the country profited greatly.

However, Child and Davenant were not convinced free traders. They supported it only in so far as it served the purpose of their Company. There was a great deal of Mercantilist doctrine in both of them ; and they have betrayed this here and there in their works. For instance, Child was in favour of restraining the trade of British plantations wholly to England, and he would discourage the importation of commodities from Venice, because of the purely bullionist reason that they were purchased with ready money. Even in the matter of the Indian trade, Child and Davenant were not prepared to accept thoroughgoing Free Trade. While condemning tariffs on imports, they held staunchly to the India Trade monoply of the Company. Their opponents repeatedly pointed out this inconsistency in them, but they never satisfactorily explained it. Cary therefore got the full advantage over them when he wrote : " The proposition that trade should be free, I allow, if it is thereby meant that trade should not be monopolised by Joint Stocks."* The Company's supporters loudly proclaimed that the Indian trade was " a great honour and advantage " to England ; but their opponents maintained that only the Company's shareholders gained, and that the nation as a whole did not benefit by it. There was then a general feeling of opposition to the Company's rigid monopoly throughout the country, and this was partly

* Bodleian § 658, No. 55.

due to its high-handedness. " These monopolisers and retailers vye with the Noblemen, hector the Gentlemen, trample upon the manufacturer and oppose everything that is for the nation's good if it cross their private interest."

There is no use enumerating the inconsistencies of Child and Davenant. They were but practical men forced by circumstances to take up a position against orthodox mercantilism. They saw the weaknesses of that system, and they had a faint glimmer of the truth of the free trade view ; yet they were but mercantilists trying to adjust that system to their convenience and self-interest. By sheer necessity they took up the free trade view, but they did not hold to it consistently ; nor had they the disposition to explore fully the implications of the new theory. This had been the case with many discoverers in other realms also. As Arnold Toynbee wrote, " original people always are confused, because they are feeling their way."* Yet it is to the credit of Child and Davenant that they made headway against the powerful bastion of mercantilism and made it possible for their successors to raze it to the ground.

IV

The Linen Drapers' Defence of Free Trade

Outside the East India Company, the linen drapers who dealt in Indian calicoes had the greatest interest in maintaining the Indian trade. During the agitation for the prohibition of Indian manufactures in 1696, Cary's *Discourse Concerning East India Trade* was put before both Houses of Parliament. † The linen drapers availed themselves of this opportunity to attack Cary's views and this produced a rather protracted controversy which was fought by means of pamphlets and broadsides. The linen drapers' attack on Cary took the form of a clever vindication of the new theory of free trade. Although their arguments were in the main

---

* Toynbee, *The Industrial Revolution*, p. 82.

† See Cary's letter to Locke, May 7, 1696. Brit. Mus. Addl. MSS. 5540. p. 72.

a restatement of earlier writings, yet they expounded the
theory more ably and with much more comprehension.
They stood for free trade in its entirety, and had none of
the reserves of the Company's supporters, who, while condemning certain restraints on Indian trade, were for tighten-
ing the monopoly enjoyed by their corporation.

The drapers argued that England's volume of commerce
would dwindle if too many restrictions were put upon it.
" Trade in general," they wrote,* " is always free, and will
never endure to be shackled and compelled, so that when
any nation or society whatever shall by unreasonable prohibitions or other means endeavour to curb and restrain it
here, it will without doubt make her uneasie in her present
residence and watch for all opportunities for repairing thither
where she is likely to meet with better quarters and kinder
treatment." If Indian calico trade was restrained in
England, that trade would pass to the Dutch and other
foreign nations. Already the Dutch were rejoicing to hear
that England was interested in prohibiting her Indian
trade.

Again, if the cheap Indian cottons and silks were prohibited in England, their place would be taken by the more
expensive linens from the Continent, and this would in no
way benefit the English nation, nor even the manufacturers
themselves. They therefore maintained, in the strain of
Davenant that " it was the interest of the nation that the
Home Consumption should be little, of a Cheap and Foreign
Growth," and that English manufactures should be sent
abroad and at the best market, because " by all that is spent
at home one loseth what another gets ; the nation is not the
richer. But a foreign consumption is clear profit, adds to
the heap without taking from the inhabitant."† This, of
course, smacks of mercantilism. No doubt they were trying
to refute mercantilist arguments by counter-arguments on
the same plane. But Cary easily turned round and refuted
them.‡ There were enough men to work in England, he said,

* Brit. Mus. 81ℓ. m. 13. No. 136.
† 816. m. 13. No. 141.
‡ *ibid*, No. 142.

and there was plenty of wool to clothe people both at home and abroad. Why then go in for foreign cloth ?

However, if once it were granted that England could not do without some linen from outside—which was indeed the case at that time—it then would follow that the drapers were right in preferring Indian calico to German linen. The weavers pointed out that this was harmful to the country, because German linen came in exchange for English woollens, while calicoes came in exchange for bullion. Already, owing to the increased use of calicoes in England, less linen came from Germany, and the export of woollen cloth to Germany also became correspondingly reduced. This was detrimental to the interest of the weavers and ultimately of the nation as a whole. The drapers, however, maintained that the leather, tin and woollens sent from England to Germany could not be got cheaper elsewhere, and so would still be bought from England. " If we take less of their linen," added the drapers,* " the balance must be paid in money and that money ought to be laid out to the best advantage. Now if calicoes were three times cheaper than linen, the question is whether we had better send one-third part of our money to India to buy calicoes or take it out in linens from Germany at treble the price."

Here the cleavage between the producers and the consumers came out in bold relief. It was certainly to the interest of the consumer to buy from the cheapest market ; but to the manufacturers the material question was whether their commodities would find a sale. Was it to the interest of the nation to buy costly German linen because it was bought in exchange for English woollens ? At that time, perhaps, some consumers, either out of blind patriotism, or from the reasoned belief that the dislocation of the woollen industry would lead ultimately to the decay of the whole country, answered that question in the affirmative ; but the drapers emphatically answered it in the negative, and perhaps the same answer would be given to-day by the majority of people in England.

The linen drapers made their views on trade even clearer

* *op. cit.* No. 143.

in their answer to the criticism that the East India trade was carried on by the exportation of bullion and did not involve the sale of English manufactures. The defence was not based on the wholesale denial that its trade harmed English industries, but came from a more correct perception of economic truths than that which obtained in their generation. " It is the interest of England," they asserted, " to send their products and manufactures to the best market and from thence to bring such commodities as they cannot purchase cheaper anywhere else (and the remainder in money) which they ought to lay out where they may buy cheapest ; and by this natural circulation the nation will be enriched."* This was perhaps too revolutionary a view for the time, but it shows that the authors of these broadsides were far in advance of the time in their knowledge of economic principles.

Nor did they leave unchallenged the position maintained by the mercantilists that protection alone could raise the price of lands and the prosperity of the people. By an effective process of reasoning they showed that prohibition would make everything dear, and that this would hinder trade and bring about its decay. On the contrary, free trade would increase wealth and population, and it was " the only way of raising the price of lands and other estates." Here is a sample of their effective reasoning : " A Free Trade makes all manner of commodities cheap ; the cheapness of commodities empowers our people to work cheaper ; the cheapness of work encourages foreign trade, and foreign trade brings wealth and people, and that alone raises the price of land and houses." Subsequent history has doubtless borne out the truth of this statement.

V

The Example of Holland

The protagonists on either side of the calico controversy drew much inspiration from other European countries. The mercantilists looked to France, where economic policy was

* *Op. cit.* No. 143.

then dominated by a rigid Colbertism, and the free-traders naturally looked to Holland, which in those days pursued a liberal economic policy. France still was the centre of civilisation ; ideas and fashions still came mainly from that country. But it was asserted by Davenant that England should not follow the Colbertian ideal of France as the economic conditions varied widely in the two countries. In France, trade was not natural, but " forced " and, therefore, much regulation was perhaps necessary ; but " in countries inclined to it (trade) by genius, such laws are needless, unnatural and can have no effect conducive to public good."* Such were England and Holland, and therefore the example of Holland was repeatedly quoted by the Company's supporters as also by the linen-drapers ; but the mercantilists as readily repudiated it as unsuited to England.

The Dutch were at that time the greatest trading nation of the world. Their ships were everywhere, and they carried goods for all nations. This made them wealthy and prosperous. Child was one of the few Englishmen who studied the conditions of Dutch trade. He begins his *Discourse of Trade* (1690) with the assertion that " the Prodigious increase of the Netherlanders in their Domestic and Foreign Trade, riches, multitudes of shipping is the envy of the present and may be the wonder of future generations." He attributes this prosperity to manifold causes, e.g., the presence of merchants in the greatest Councils of State and of War, their system of inheritance, according to which the father's property was divided equally between the sons, encouragement of inventions and shipping, and the spread of education irrespective of sex and class. A warm admirer of the Dutch, Child was also an ardent advocate for the emulation of their example by England.

Trade was free in Holland, and this also was pointed out as a cause of its prosperity. When calico first came into the country, the Dutch were afraid that it would harm their linen industry, and prohibited it. Thereby the calico trade was lost to Holland, and England took her place. The

* Works I, p. 99.

Dutch were shrewd enough to see their mistake, and soon removed the prohibition, after which their trade increased by leaps and bounds. It was thus that the Dutch, " of a Poor and Distressed people, became the High and Mighty of the World in less than a hundred years, and that under the great disadvantage of a very chargeable country."* The Company and the linen drapers urged that the free trade policy of Holland must be followed in England also.

Cary strongly opposed this view. Holland may have prospered under free trade, but the same policy may ruin England, because the conditions of the two countries were different according to him. " The interest of Holland in trade is but one single interest ; they live by buying and selling, and thus trade of course does well enough there, because being a great number of people met together on a small plot of land and having no product of their own, they furnish each other with what they want which being all fetch'd from abroad employs great numbers of bulky ships, which they sail cheap and are therefore enabled also to supply other parts of Flanders with such commodities whereof they have an overplus above their own consumption ; so that Holland is now become a magazine of Trade and Commerce, and therefore they raise their taxes by methods which shall oblige all temporary residents to pay towards the support of the Government, for which reason they give greater immunities in trade than the circumstances of England will admit." Holland can afford to make trade thus free because they have only the traders' interest to consider ; they have little land to improve. " In England," continues Cary, " we have two interests, that of the freeholder and that of the trader, and these are in themselves of different natures." Both these interests must be harmonised in framing a trade policy for England. A free trade may benefit the trader, but it might ruin the landowner and the manufacturer. Hence the laws restraining the exportation of wool and the importation of cheap corn.

The linen drapers insisted that there was no essential difference between England and Holland. If England had

* 816. m. 13. No. 143.

lands to improve, so had Holland. They maintained that free trade did not harm the landed interest ; it ultimately would increase the value of land and houses. But this view was too difficult for the average man to agree to ; nor was it possible under the circumstances of the time to demonstrate the truth of this view.

The fundamental difference between the mercantilists and the linen drapers turned upon the question whether or not England should become like Holland—a nation of traders. The former wanted to combine the interests of industries with those of trade ; they even wanted to make trade the handmaid of industry. Cary, although a merchant, insisted that England should look first to the interest of her home industries, because they secured employment for the people and increased national wealth. But the linen drapers stood for a forward policy in foreign trade. As they put it emphatically :—" We say we are an island better accommodated and more immediately depending on trade . . . than Holland itself. Our ships are our walls, our trade our riches. We are situated by nature to be the mart of Europe. It is the restraint upon us (because England is not a free port) that all trade doth not centre here. To prohibit the use of foreign manufactures, were still to do us further mischief ; this would render our shipping useless and lessen our navigation ; and in our Naval Force lies not only the welfare but the very Being of our Nation."* They agreed that national industries must be fostered, but the best way of doing so was " to leave trade free and shelter it against all prohibitions."

The cleavage of opinion above noticed has always been at the root of the controversy between Protection and Free Trade. The Protectionist position had been previously expounded *ad nauseum ;* but the Free Trade view had never been put more cogently than by the linen drapers. England's unique position as a trading power was fully grasped by them. Whatever may have been thought of their views by contemporaries, they have been amply vindicated by subsequent history.

* 816. m. 13. No. 141.

VI

Thorough-going Free Trade

The best exposition of the Free Trade view during the period (and perhaps until the time of Adam Smith) is contained in the *Considerations upon the East India Trade*, an anonymous tract of eighty pages first published in 1701.* It contains a spirited, but well-reasoned protest against protectionism and allied aspects of mercantilist policy. It has been highly commended by McCulloch and Macaulay, and the latter even thought that the tracts of Davenant were contemptible in comparison. Nevertheless modern writers have almost completely disregarded this valuable tract. † Sir William Ashley, in his illuminating survey of early free trade, does not even mention it, and yet this was the best statement of the Free Trade view in the period covered by him. ‡

The writer begins with an enunciation of method which is commendable for that period. " Instead of using only comparative and superlative words to amuse the reader," our author has endeavoured " to express himself in terms of number, weight and measure " ; and he " would not speak with confidence of anything that is not as certain as the very principles of geometry."

The *Considerations* does not look like a mere partisan pamphlet. It is written in a scientific spirit and surveys many of what we now consider the fundamental questions of economics. The nature of money and wealth, of trade and credit ; the results of prohibitions and protective duties ; the conditions and results of division of labour and the application of machinery ;—these are some of the topics dealt with in it. We have unfortunately no space

---

* It was republished in 1720 under the changed title, *Advantages of the East India Trade to England Considered*, but with no modifications in the text. The Goldsmith's Library contains copies of both.

† It is mentioned by Dr. Marshall (*Industries and Trade*, p. 713), E. Lipson (*Woollen and Worsted Industries*, p. 38) and S. Bauer (Dict. Pol. Econ. I, p. 87), but Dr. Bauer misconstrues the purport of the work, and regards it as greatly mingled with Mercantilist beliefs.

‡ *Surveys Historic and Economic* (1900) pp. 268-303.

for dealing with all these topics ; we shall examine here only its exposition of the free trade view.

It first analyses the nature of foreign trade, and begins by examining the familiar bullionist fallacy. Why do we send bullion to India in exchange for calicoes and silks ? Because these goods are more valuable to us than the bullion sent for them ; because they are cheaper than if they were made in this country. In technical language the author puts it as *the exchange of greater for less value.* This he regards as the natural basis of foreign trade. He proves scientifically that this natural flow of goods from country to country is advantageous for all parties. Here is his reasoning :—" If nine (men) cannot produce above three bushels of wheat in England, if by equal labour they might procure nine bushels from another country, to imploy these in agriculture at home is to imploy nine to do no more work than might be done as well by three ; is to imploy six to do no more work than might be done as well without them ; is to imploy six to no profit which might be imploy'd to procure as many bushels of wheat to England ; is the loss of six bushels of wheat ; is therefore the loss of so mnch value. So if nine by so much labour can make in England a manufacture but of the value of 10 shillings, if by equal labour they can procure from other countries thrice as much value of manufactures, to imploy these men in English Manufacture is to imploy to no profit six of the nine which might be imploy'd to procure twice as much value of manufactures from abroad, is clearly the loss of so much value to the nation."*

He condemns emphatically the policies of protection and prohibition. To him they were based upon wrong calculations and misconceptions. " Manufactures made in England the like of which may be imported from East-Indies by the labour of fewer hands, are not profitable ; they are a loss to the kingdom ; the Publick therefore loses nothing by the loss of such Manufactures."† More than that. It is an unjustifiable waste " to provide for our

---

* pp. 55-56. (The page references are to the Edition of 1701.)
† p. 56.

consumption by the labour of many which might as well
be done by that of the few." A people who practise such
extravagance are " fit for Bedlam." He dilates upon the
evils of starting industries unsuited to the country. Such
manufactures will be " too dear for foreign markets," and—
this is significant—" by having less to do in Foreign Markets,
we shall have so much the less imployment for our people
here at home." This is very modern indeed.

Many writers in that period condemned restrictions
on trade, but no other work before *The Wealth of Nations*
gives such an acute analysis of the nature of protection and
free trade. Our author has constructed a system of his
own, and he " builded better than he knew."

Effective in whatever he writes, he grows eloquent when
he speaks of the advantages of foreign trade to England.
" Why are we surrounded with the sea ? Surely that our
wants at home might be supplied by our navigation with
other countries, the least and easiest labour. By this we
taste the spices of Arabia, yet we never feel the scorching
sun that brings them forth. We shine in silks which our
hands have not wrought. . . . We only plough the
deep and reap the harvest of every country in the
world."*

Continuing on the ultimate results of the importation
of Indian goods, the author hits upon some of the fundamental principles of the modern industrial system. He
for the first time brings out the complicated relationship
between division of labour, extent of market, prices, wages
and other allied factors in production. Competition
with Indian cottons and silks would make it essential that
English manufactures should be made as cheap. Manufacturers will then strain every nerve to introduce economies
in their business and will hit upon labour-saving engines
and other cheaper methods of production. Further, when
prices are reduced, there will be a greater demand for goods,
and this will bring about a more minute division of labour.
This will reduce the price still more, and thereby further
increase the market. Yet the wages of the workers will

* pp. 58-89.

not go down. " Without abating the *wages of the labourer*
it may well abate the *price of labour.*"* He himself calls
this a " paradox " in production.

The author is, however, no arm-chair theorist ; he
appeals to the experience of his readers for proof of his statements. He takes effective illustrations from the making
of ships, watches, clothes, etc. Here is one of them. " A
watch is a work of great variety ; it is possible for one artist
to make all the several Parts and at least to join them all
together ; but if the Demand of Watches should become as
very great as to find constant imployment for as many
Persons as there are Parts in a Watch, if to everyone shall
be assigned his proper and constant work, if one shall have
nothing else to make but Cases, another Weels, another
Pins, another Screws, and several others their proper Parts ;
and lastly if it shall be the constant and only imployment
of one to join these several Parts together, this Man must
needs be more skilful and expeditious in the composition
of these several Parts than the same Man cou'd be if he
were also to be imploy'd in the Manufacture of all these Parts.
And so the Maker of the Pins, or Wheels, or Screws, or other
Parts must needs be more perfect and expeditious at his
proper work, if he shall have nothing else to push and com-
found his skill, than if he is also to be imploy'd in all the
variety of the Watch."† One may compare this with
similar passages of Adam Smith, and yet may not find
much to the advantage of the latter.

He makes a spirited defence of the application of
mechanical methods in production and forcibly condemns
the popular opposition to such improvements. To him it
was folly to resist labour-saving methods. Here is one of
his examples :—" Five men in a barge upon a navigable
River will carry as much as a hundred times so many horses
upon the land ; if the navigation of the River shall be
neglected that the same carriage may be performed by hand
nineteen in twenty of these men and all these horses are
more than are necessary to do the work, so many are imploy'd

* p. 72.
† pp. 69-70.

to do the work that may be done as well without them."
Although the author lived long before the era of Industrial
Revolution, he seems to have had a vision into the future
possibilities of mechanical improvements and their influence
on the economic life of the people. "Arts, and Mills, and
Engines, which save the labour of Hands are ways of doing
things with less labour and consequently with labour of less
price though the Wages of Men imploy'd to do them shou'd
not be abated . . . ; such things are successively
invented to do a great deal of work with little labour of
hands ; they are the effects of necessity and emulation ;
. . . if my neighbour, by doing much with little labour,
can sell cheap, I must continue to sell as cheap as he ; so
that every art, trade or engine doing work with labour of
fewer hands and consequently cheaper begets in others
a kind of necessity and emulation either of using the same
art, trade or engine or of inventing something like it, that
every man may be upon the square, that no man may be
able to undersell his neighbour."* One would hardly think
that these words were written in 1700.

Space does not permit any more extracts from the tract
under review, and perhaps it will be possible to form a
general estimate of the work from what has been given
above. The *Considerations* was the first work to tackle
some of the fundamental questions of economics in a
scientific spirit. For the first time it gave a theoretical
basis to the claim of freedom from restraint in foreign trades.
That work also first brought out the complex interactions
between prices and wages, between cost of production and
extent of market. Long before Adam Smith, it demonstrated
that " the division of labour is limited by the extent of the
market," and it analysed the economic results of mechanical
inventions. At a time when people had hazy notions of
credit, the author grasped its true nature and realised its
function in economic life. Nor is the tract dull reading ;
it is enlivened by a rich and forcible style, a language never
vague, a presentation that sustains the interest of the reader
in spite of frequent repetitions. It is head and shoulders

* pp. 66-67.

above the economic writings of that age ; and it doubtless deserves a place among the masterpieces of English Political Economy.

The authorship of this tract is a puzzle. That such a weighty work should come out anonymously is rather strange. In the catalogue of the British Museum and in Halket and Laing's Dictionary, it is tentatively attributed to Sir Dudley North.* But North died (1691) many years before the incidents given in the tract took place. Besides his known writings do not by any means warrant this identification. McCulloch and the authorities above named mention also that the tract was often attributed to Henry Martyn (died 1721) ; on various grounds it seems highly probable that Henry Martyn was the author of the tract, and in an appendix the question is further discussed. Martyn is a talented writer, and is the author of many well-known papers. Moreover, he was a Whig, and this fact is specially noteworthy because it raises a very important question regarding the relation of the free trade view with the political parties

VII

Was Free Trade of Tory Origin ?

After an examination of the pamphlet literature of the late seventeenth and early eighteenth centuries, Sir William Ashley came to the conclusion that there was a " natural " connection between the Tory party and the advocacy of the Free Trade view. † A survey of the same sources by the present writer makes him seriously doubt that there was any such natural connection. If any connection existed it must have been accidental, and does not justify the conclusion that free trade was Tory in origin.

* *Dictionary of Anonymous and Pseudonymous Literature of Great Britain*, p. 471. This view is accepted by T. E. Gregory in *Economica*, January, 1921, p. 45, 48.

† *Surveys Historic and Economic* (1900), pp. 268-303. This view has been accepted also by Cûnningham (Modern Times, pp. 406, and 456-57.).

PROTECTIONISM *versus* FREE TRADE

The view of Professor Ashley looks rather paradoxical, seeing that the Tories, representing the landed interest, were in those days regarded as hating trade. As Trevelyan has pointed out, they were afraid that foreign trade would turn England into another Holland—i.e., a trading republic. Such a party could hardly be expected to oppose the imposition of restraints on trade. Indeed, nothing must have been more hateful to the Tories than a Free Trade policy.

It is true that in the controversy on the French trade the Tory party for a time identified itself with a more liberal trade policy than that pursued by the Whigs ; but this was accidental, and fleeting. As has been shown in another connection, the issues were more political than economic. Alarmed at the French sympathies of Charles II and the possible evils of a Catholic revival in England, the Whigs moved for a total prohibition of the French import trade. The main economic issue involved was not so much the anxiety to protect native industries as the fear of the mercantilists that France was rapidly draining England of her treasure. The Tories did not approve of this policy, and supported the king, not because they wanted to have free trade with France, but because they knew that absolute prohibition would rob the king's treasury of much revenue. They did not disapprove of protective tariffs on French imports, and even the royalist Parliament of James II kept up those high tariffs in the interests of English industries.

Thus in the French trade dispute, many different issues were confused, and all were dominated by the political motive. But in the controversy on the Indian trade there was one clear economic issue—viz., Protectionism *versus* Free Trade ; and this naturally served as a better touchstone for testing the trade views of the two political parties. Not only do we fail to see any definite cleavage between them on this question, but we see abundant signs of agreement as to the need of protecting home industries against Indian exports. The Tory party did not signify the least adherence to the free trade view. No doubt, owing to the indefatigable exertions of the Directors of the East India

Company (who happened to be Tories) to gain support for their cause, many members of Parliament were won over against the Prohibition Bills on 1696-97 and even in 1699-1700 ; but this made little difference. As a matter of fact, most of the humiliations of the Company after 1689 came when Tories were in power, and this is very significant.

The truth of the matter is that there was as yet no definite party cleavage on the question of Protection *versus* Free Trade. Officially both parties were on the whole for Government regulation of trade in the interests of the home producer, and if some men of either party gave up this traditional view in relation to one particular trade it was either due to self-interest or because they by their individual observation saw the truth of the opposite position. Self-interest, however, was the predominant motive. The first supporters of the free trade view were the trading companies, because it was evidently their interest to carry on import trade unimpeded by prohibitions and protective duties. It was thus that Child and Davenant turned to free trade, and they did so only to the extent that it favoured the East India Company's interests. North was a merchant of the Turkey Company, and rose to be the leading English merchant in Constantinople. The linen drapers were evidently interested in obtaining foreign linen cheap, and naturally they opposed high tariffs. At the same time, other commercial bodies, clamoured for protective measures, because such a policy was thought more suitable for their particular interests. Thus it was self-interest that shaped the trade views of various individuals and trading bodies, and it is a mistake to connect their views with the political parties to which they happened to belong. The free trade view of Henry Martyn had little to do with his Whiggism ; still less was the Toryism of Child and Davenant responsible for their views on trade. Trade was primarily the concern of business classes, and they ranged themselves on opposite sides when their interests collided. Besides the constitution of the two political parties at that time was such as not to allow them to identify themselves with either view. The present party cleavage on tariff policy dates from much later times. If the Tories in 1713 proposed to reduce tariff on French imports, the Whig premier, Walpole, in 1721 made great reductions in tariffs on both exports and imports. The whole question therefore needs to be revised in the light of facts.

Chapter V

THE PROHIBITION OF INDIAN TEXTILE IMPORTS.

I

First Attempts at Legislation

WITH the Glorious Revolution of 1688, the East India Company lost its royal patronage. The Company, having been a Court favourite, Parliament looked upon it with suspicion and hostility. Sir Josia Child, the uncrowned king of the Company, was a very influential person, and knew how to humour those who were in power. But Child was a Tory, and he had many enemies like Papillon in the Whig party. Those enemies had long been looking for an opportunity to humiliate him, and they found it soon after the Glorious Revolution, when the Whigs came into power. Child for a time was over-matched. After 1692 the Company was attacked both in England and India by various coteries of interlopers who carried on private trade under the connivance of Parliament ; nay, its very existence was imperilled by the incorporation of a rival Company backed up by Government. The protracted struggle that ensued, and the dramatic incidents connected with it, have been vividly sketched by Sir William Hunter and Mr. P. E. Roberts* ; and those need not be recounted here.

Misfortunes never come single, and so it was with the Company. For a long time the onslaught against the Indian Trade was averted by " the arts of the great Goliah," but after 1690 these arts were not so effective as before. What with the energetic activity of the Company and of the numerous interlopers, there was a large increase in the

* *The History of British India*, Vol. II.

quantity of Indian silks and calicoes imported into England. The use of Indian cloth spread among all sorts and conditions of people, and this led to the increased displacement of English woollens and silks. The weavers were exasperated more than ever, and their groans and moans became audible everywhere. Great hopes were roused among them when the Whig party came back to power in 1695. No doubt the Whigs had a private spite against the Company, but whether they were opposed to calico trade on principle had yet to be tested. The weavers hardly realised then that calico traders, whether Whigs or Tories, had the same interest, however much they differed in other matters. However the weavers found favour with that remarkable body called the Commissioners of Trade and Plantations. John Pollexfen, one of that body, took up their cause in right earnest.

In 1696, the Companies of silk weavers at Canterbury, the worsted weavers at Norwich, the say-makers and worsted yarn makers of Norfolk and Cambridge,* sent up petitions to the House of Commons stating that their manufactures had fallen into a most pitiable condition owing to the general wear of East India silks and calicoes. The petitions were favourably received, and were referred to a Committee, with Sir Henry Hobart as Chairman. The petitioners proved their case before this Committee through their representatives and counsel. John Carter and Metcalfe, on behalf of the Canterbury Weavers, proved that " the manufacture of silk was brought to such a perfection . . . (as to) cope with any market in the world save that of East Indies." The worsted and woollen manufacturers were even more successful in bringing home the justice of their complaints. The Norwich weavers claimed that 100,000 persons depended upon their " manufactory " which used up annually wool to the value of £200,000. The rise in the price of wool from 16s. to 40s. per tod, they said, was due to the prosperity of their industries. Similarly the manufacturers of Suffolk and Cambridge pointed out that they employed 40,000 persons, and that by their prosperity " the poor people take

* *House of Commons Journals*, XI, pp. 496-97.

their children from the highways and their infant idleness ; and bring them to Wool and Wheel whereat one of five years of age will earn 4d a day." Both companies cleverly insinuated that wool-growers were greatly affected by the progress or decay of their industries. They pointed out that "the East India trade had so much influence over wool in England that the price thereof rises and falls with the scarcity and glut of the Company's said commodities." The latter Company's assertion that "even accidental disappointments to the East India Company" suddenly raised the prospects of wool and woollen industries, was certainly calculated to touch the interests of the classes that then dominated Parliament. The Committee resolved that the petitioners had proved their point to their satisfaction, and that a Bill should be brought to restrain the wearing of Indian textile goods. Hobart himself was commissioned to draw up a Bill.

On March 10th, the Bill* was presented to the House. It prohibited not only "all wrought silks, Bengalls, dyed, printed or stained callicoes of the product of India or Persia or any place within the charter of the East India Company which shall be imported into this Kingdom," but also those "*that are or shall be dyed, printed or stained in this kingdom or elsewhere.*" All these goods should henceforth be exported again, and not worn in England. Any one bartering or selling these goods should "forfeit £100 for every offence, one moiety thereof for the use of the poor of the parish where the offence was committed and the other moiety for those who sue for the same."

The Bill had a prosperous course in the House of Commons, but it is impossible to ascertain the exact details of it. The formal statements entered in the Journals do not help us very much in forming an idea of the debate that ensued, and Cobbett's *Parliamentary History* hardly mentions this Bill. Charles Montague was then Chancellor of the Exchequer, and his grip of financial problems had gained him an ascendancy in the House which was unsurpassed until the ministry of the younger Pitt. The

* *Commons Journals*, XI.

originator of various important fiscal arrangements, he has been not unsuitably called " the founder of the financial system of the Revolution."* He was a strong believer in a protective tariff and even prohibition, and we can see his hand in the economic policy towards Ireland and the French and India trades. It was under his influence that two successive bills were introduced in Parliament to prohibit Indian goods, and if both the bills failed it was because of some inexplicable manœuvre in the Upper House and the eventual cropping up of a vital constitutional question. Yet Montague persisted in urging the point, and got it passed in 1700 in a Parliament of independent Whigs and Tories hostile to himself as well as to the king. There is a tradition reported in *Chronicon Rusticum Commerciale* (1747) † on the authority of a pamphlet of 1743, that Montague later regretted his part in the prohibition of Indian textiles, and that he told a person of credit (who told the author) that " in his lifetime he had never done anything which he so sincerely repented of." The judicious John Smith discredited this story. Besides, Montague's part in opposing the trade clauses in the treaty of Utrecht also makes us doubt the truth of that report.

On March 31, the Bill came before the House of Lords. Already they had received various papers (in connection with the dispute about the Scottish India Company), one of which was from John Pollexfen, against the Indian textile trade. ‡ Pollexfen used all the force of his arguments and all the weight of his official position to make out a strong case against the importation of calicoes and silks into England. The arguments of Pollexfen were answered by papers, similarly submitted, by Shelden and by the East India Company. The Company's defence was saturated with Child's ideas and peculiar expressions and was probably drawn up by him. It based its claim on *laissez faire* arguments. Shelden made out a rather feeble case.

* Lecky, *History of England in the Eighteenth Century*, Vol. I, p. 144.
† Vol. II, p. 46, footnote.
‡ Hist. MSS. Comm., New Series, VII, pp. 44-60.

MERCANTILISM AND THE EAST INDIA TRADE

From the first day of April the Lords heard counsel for both sides, and received numerous petitions from interested parties.* Not only woollen, worsted and silk manufacturers, but various industrial classes whose trade was harmed by the Indian imports petitioned that the Bill was absolutely necessary for their security. The japanners complained that the lacquered ware imported by the East India Company had ruined their "mistery and manufacture," which on their own showing excelled in the imitation of Eastern methods."† The Company of " Joiners " inveighed against the importation of cabinets and allied goods from India.‡ The fan-makers had severe grievances against Indian fans and fansticks which were being increasingly imported into England.§ They had built up a prosperous business in fan-making, varnishing and painting with the help of materials imported from Turkey and Russia. But as 550,000 Indian fans had been sold in England at low prices, their manufacture was threatened with extinction. All these various classes had real grievances, and indeed deserved the sympathy of Parliament.

The opposition to the Bill came from those who sold or worked up Indian goods for the English market, and there was quite a numerous class of people engaged in such work. Prominent among these were the linen drapers and calico-printers, but there were also minor trades like calenderers, upholsterers, calico-dyers and stainers. The linen drapers sent up many petitions with numerous signatures, and were represented by Sir Thomas Powys and Sir Bartholomew Shore. Powys figures frequently in the Parliamentary Journals of the time, and was apparently a prominent lawyer of the day, but his contention that " the weavers are as full of employment as ever known " did not carry much conviction to the House. Petitions also came from callenderers of London, from the shopkeepers and warehouse keepers trading in East India silks and

* H. MSS. Comm., Vol. II, No. 1050.
† Brit. Mus., 816. m. 13. (1).
‡ *Ibid* (2).
§ 816. m. 12 (97).

calicoes, from several merchants of London exporting East India goods to the West Indies, and from a very important section of people called "gentlemen's sons apprentices of Linen drapers . . . . whose guardians had lent considerable sums to the Masters,"* and 281 signatures were affixed to this. The principal contention of the dealers in Indian goods was that the Bill would ruin their flourishing business, in which thousands were employed. Many of them had vast stocks of East India goods, which would not sell if the Bill passed. William Arnold told the House that he had in stock calicoes to the value of £10,000. It was also alleged that the time allowed for disposing of the goods was too short, and calicoes would still remain and rot in their shops and warehouses. The interests of these classes and the East India Company were thus almost the same ; yet there seems to have been no concerted action among them. The drapers had various complaints against the monopolistic methods of the Company, and petitioned Parliament more than once against its "ill-conduct . . . . in artificially raising the price of Indian goods." There was therefore no love lost between the linen drapers and the Company, and the former had alone to fight their quarrel with Cary and others. The drapers also declared for an open trade with India,† and this widened the gulf that separated the two parties.

The petitioners against the Bill included also calico-printers and stainers, calico and linen dyers, silk dyers, glazers, buckram-stiffeners and a host of other tradesmen. Nor were they few in numbers. Thomas Kettle told the House that there were thousands employed in dyeing and calendering alone. Their prayer was to delete the clause (above under-lined) prohibiting the use of even calicoes printed and worked up in England. They were represented by at least three lawyers, Jekyll, Pooley and Dyer. Jekyll claimed that calico-printing was "as much a manufacture as any woollen" and deserved encouragement. Pooley said that his clients were a numerous people, and he used Davenants' arguments

* *Op. cit.*, p. 243.
† *Commons Journals*, XI, p. 31.

that the cheapness of calico and its home consumption were advantageous to the kingdom. The calico-printers seem to have spent a good deal to further their cause. One of them confessed before the House subsequently that he spent £200 in fees to solicitors and others.* Some of them appeared before the House and stoutly opposed the clause that was calculated to ruin their trade. William Sherwin said that the trade employed 400 people. Kettle, a dyer, said that if calicoes were prohibited his people would starve. There were also other minor trades that depended upon calico-dyeing. Thomas Symonds said that dyers used his log-wood and indigo, which would no more be the case when calico was prohibited. On the whole these traders made out a rather strong case against the inclusion of calico-printed in England into the operation of the Bill, and when it finally passed in 1700, that clause was not included. We will follow later the fortunes of the calico-printing industry.†

It is indeed surprising how many minor industries arose to supplement the East India trade—all depending upon it and claiming special recognition at the hands of the legislature. Much of it was probably due to the alarm raised by the Company, and even their petitions were probably drawn up by its men. There was especially one petition in which the Company's hand is visible—that of the packers and cloth-workers of Gloucestershire who provided woollen goods to the Company.‡ They were brought forward to show that even a section of the woollen manufacture was interested in the continuance of the East India trade.

On April 17, it was proposed to make an immediate report, but it was negatived under some inexplicable influence. The Bill was amended in Committee, and the printed calicoes were excluded from the operation of the Bill, and " Bengalls " omitted altogether. We do not know what further proceedings took place after this. The editors of the House of Lords Records laconically say " No further proceedings

* *Commons Journals*, V., XI, p. 683.
† See Chapter IV.
‡ A similar petition in 1693, Dec., *Commons Journals*, XI, p. 41.

recorded." According to the pamphlet above quoted,* the Bill was not passed by the Lords. Evidently, the House of Lords was then dominated by Tory magnates, and the East India Company must have somehow influenced the leading members, some of whom had shares in the Company.

The weavers were touched to the quick. Agitators excited their passions by scurrillous ballads against the " Great Goliah," and the Company. When passion was at its height, there came a great sale at the East India House, when vast quantities of silks and calicoes were disposed of.† This made a commotion in the city, and the weavers were desperate. On the very same day, some hundreds of silk weavers " went in a body to Westminster " to petition the Parliament against the East India imports. Their procession through the city caused great sensation, especially in Leadenhall Street. Several hundred men went to Westminster the next day also. The newspapers of the time record these incidents in their scanty columns. ‡

II

The Bill of 1697

The House of Commons soon realised the situation and took up the question a second time. On November 30, Sir Henry Hobart and Mr. Blofield were commissioned to prepare a fresh Bill to restrain the free import of Indian calicoes and silks.§ A Bill on the same lines as that of the previous year was drawn up and read for the first time on December 4. Soon after this, petitions poured in from various industrial centres in the Eastern Counties. The principal ones were from London, Norwich, Canterbury, Whitechapel, Bury St. Edmunds, the French Refugees,

* *A True Relation* . . . *East India Company.*

† November 24, 1696, Narcissus Luttrell's *Brief Relation of the State of Affairs*, 1678-1714, Vol. IV, 144.

‡ *The Protestant Mercury*, Nov. 25 ; *The Post Boy*, Nov. 26 (Nichols' Newspapers, Bodl.).

§ *Commons Journals*, XI ; Luttrell, p. 147.

Mile End, Newtown, Worcester, Rumsey and Gloucester-shire. Some of them were drawn up on slender grounds. For example, the clothrash-makers of Rumsey complained that the Company had not been for some time past buying their rash. The clothiers of Gloucestershire also petitioned for the Bill as the East India trade had stopped their exports to Turkey† ; and it is noteworthy that about the same time the cloth-workers and packers of that very place petitioned the Lords against the Bill, as they were employed in providing goods to the Company.* Among the petitions before the Commons there was only one against the Bill, and that came from the linen drapers (December 10). It is significant that no petitions were received from the Company.

The Bill was read a second time on December 30. An amendment was proposed bringing stuffs mixed with silk and herbs under the operation of the Bill. It was passed by 119 against 98. Nothing more was done for some time. On the 20th, further consideration of the Bill was adjourned a seven-night " and nothig to intervene." Why such a policy was resorted to, we are unable to ascertain.

This latter resolution however caused misgivings among those interested, and a rumour was afloat that the Bill was thrown out and that the members of the House had been bribed for it. This rumour spread like wild-fire. On January 21, the Weavers of Spitalfields " came in a body to the number of 5,000 including men, women and children, praying in a rude manner that the bill passe."† Women seem to have been at the bottom of the rising. They subscribed a halfpenny each and got together half-a-crown to hire a woman to ring the tocsin. This woman later confessed, according to Luttrell, that she " was hired for half-a-crown by another woman a Roman Catholick," who, it would appear, was prosecuted subsequently. The weavers' wives caused great trouble at the Parliament House. According to Mr. William Fleming, who was himself guarding the door, they got into the lobby and pressed so hard to go into the House

---

* H. MSS. Com., House of Lords MSS., New series, II, pp. 243-63.
† Luttrell, *op. cit.*, p. 172.

that it was difficult to keep them out. The doors were locked up. " Those members who had been against the Bill were in great fear, but those who were for it might pass and repass at pleasure."* The *Protestant Mercury*, (January 22) wrote that the weavers incurred the displeasure of the House of Commons, and that on learning this they went back to their homes without causing any further trouble. † The House of Lords was alarmed and sent for sheriffs, Justices of the Peace and constables to watch and keep peace, and ordered the trained bands of Westminster to be up the next day.

The weavers, though afraid to incur the displeasure of Parliament, wanted however to show their hatred against the East India Company. ‡ On their way back to Spitalfields, they stopped at Leadenhall Street and endeavoured to force their way into the East India House. They broke open the outer door and demolished some windows and railings. Fortunately for the Company, the Lord Mayor and the Sheriffs came to its help and forcibly dispersed the crowd. Three of the assailants were committed to Newgate prison.

The next day, January 22, four trained bands attended the Parliament House. The weavers did not dare to come again, but they gathered together in small knots in the city and tore up calicoes and silks kept for sale in the shops.§

The directors of the Company‖ were alarmed and on the same day they met to concert measures for defending their house and treasure. Some directors were commissioned to wait upon the Mayor and the Sheriffs to express the gratitude of the Court " for their great pains and troubles," and for appointing a guard of soldiers for their security. Various sums were voted by the Court : twenty guineas to the Sheriff's officers, three guineas to Mr. Field, " Officer of the

---

* Fleming's letter is printed in the Twelfth Report of the Hist. MSS. Commission, Part VII, p. 346. See also W. Foster, *The East India House*, pp. 70-71 ; S. A. Khan, *The East India Trade in the Seventeenth Century*, p. 289, note 1.

† Bodleian Collection.

‡ *Protestant Mercury, Ibid.*

§ The *Flying Post*, Jan. 23.

‖ Court Minutes, Vol. XXXVII, p. 286-87.

Poultry Country who was knocked down by the rabble and lost his hat and halbeard at their first onslaught." Sir Owen Buckingham had spent forty shillings to disperse the rabble, and he was reimbursed. The directors soon met again to "consider the best ways and means for strengthening the gate and doors of the House and securing the treasure, books of account, and what else relates to the interests of the general Joint Stock of the Company."

The Company of Weavers* dissociated themselves entirely from the rising, and in order to show their abhorrence of it they passed a bye-law to disfranchise and never more to employ those journeymen and apprentices who in future took part " in such tumultuous proceedings."

The weavers' rising had certainly some effect, for within a week the Bill was engrossed and in the next it was passed by the House. However it passed by the very narrow majority of one (140 against 139), and perhaps this was due to the changed feelings in the House.

Sent to the House of Lords on February 6, the Bill† was very favourably received by the House. Apparently they wanted to do something drastic to redress the grievances of the weavers ; but there are reasons to suspect the integrity of their intentions. There was a regular hearing of witnesses and counsel as before. A remarkable petition was received from the " Churchwardens and Overseers of the Poor and Ancient Inhabitants " of the Hamlet of Bethnal Green (Stepney), in which was stated the dire sufferings of weavers who " were reduced to such extremities as to eat horse-flesh and grains to support nature." Powys represented the linen drapers this time also, and said to the Lords that if Indian goods were prohibited the same would come from other countries. Many lawyers argued for the Bill, chiefly Phipps, Gardiner and Barrey. Captain Lekens laid it down that a trade like the East Indian that did not export English manufactures was positively harmful to the Kingdom. The Lords considered the Bill, and made twelve amendments in it. The two principal ones were (1) the inclusion of

* Luttrel, p. 177.
† H. Comm. MSS., II, p. 509.

wrought silks imported from every other country in the operation of the Bill, and (2) the penalising of wearing as well as selling the prohibited goods. The amendments were sent to the lower House for assent ; but it* was not in a mood to give heed to those modifications. The amendments were read one by one, and emphatically rejected. A conference with the Lords was desired, and a Committee including Charles Montague and Hobart was appointed to draw up reasons for dissent.

The reasons formulated by them were to the effect that (1) because the foreign wrought silks prohibited by the Lords were the produce of our manufacture (i.e., imported in exchange for our manufactured goods) the prohibition of those goods might endanger the loss of a considerable part of our foreign trade. (2) The penalty of £100 on those who wear the prohibited goods would subject persons of all qualities to the inconvenience of searches and vexatious disputes, and therefore selling alone could be penalised, and (3) that " the right of the Commons ' that all charges of money on the people should first begin in their House ' was so plain and clear and so essentially necessary to the constitution that it had been so fully settled between the two Houses and so frequently acquiesced in by the Lords." To this the Lords replied that (1) the prohibition of Indian silks alone would be quite ineffective without prohibiting other foreign silks which were equally harmful, (2) that the law to be effectual should penalise wearing as well as selling the prohibited stuffs, and (3) that they had not imposed any special charge on the people and that they did not wish to question the rights of the lower House.

The Conference was held in the Painted Chamber on March 5, and at this the above reasons were communicated mutually. The Lords did not give way and the Commons considered the Lords' Amendments again, and severally rejected them as before. One of the Commons' representatives, Sir Samuel Barnardiston†, argued in favour of the

---

* *Commons Journals*, XI, February 25th 1697.
† Luttrel, IV, p. 177.

Lords at the Conference, and he was taken to task for it by the House. However he was only reprimanded by the Speaker " in consideration of his great age and infirmities and of his sufferings and services."*

A free conference was then desired with the Lords, and both parties, while explaining their reasons more in detail, stoutly held to their original contentions. The Commons finally laid down that " no amendment how reasonable soever could be debated whereby any penalty was extended further than in the Bill," and that since " all the amendments of the Upper House related to penalties . . . . it would be very dangerous to dispute so fundamental a point, there remaining nothing for the Lords but by receding from the amendment." The Bill was therefore dropped, though both Houses were apparently for the Bill.

It is difficult not to question the *bona fides* of the House of Lords in this case. The Commons seem to have really meant to prohibit the import and use of Indian calicoes and silks. The Lords tried to make it appear that they were also for such legislation, but this is hardly convincing. Reading between the lines of their reasons for the amendments, one would naturally conclude that the Lords wanted to make use of the opportunity to revive their old claim to amend finance bills and thereby to create a precedent if possible. But this was not all. They also wanted to help the cause of the Company, in which some of them were deeply interested. At the Conference they tried to maintain that Indian silks were, like other foreign silks, " in great part the produce of our manufactures."† Those who had the interest of the Company at heart knew that the substantial amendments made by the Lords would be resented by the Commons. Nor were the Commons so much interested in the Bill as to give up their constitutional right. We do not know what hand Sir Josia Child had in the matter ; nor do we know whether the jibe of " Prince Butler " about the great Goliah's " pouring gold in plenteous showers in ladyes' laps who bore great powers " had any reference to the transactions

---

* *Commons Journals*, XI, March 20.
† *Commons Journals*, XI, p. 755.

of 1697. Anyway the Company gained its cause, and the poor weavers lost theirs.

But the weavers were not subdued. They were made desperate by the delays of Parliament, and they did not care at all for the constitutional point. King William's gift* of £2,000 to them did something to relieve their misery; but their fury against the Company was not a bit abated. On March 22, three thousand weavers got together in Spitalfields, near Hackney, and threatened Sir Josia Child's house at Wanstead.† Child was of course influential with Government and the guards came to his rescue. The soldiers fired at the mob; one was killed and others wounded. The press-masters carried several young fellows on board. Lord Lucas and the sheriffs by their prudent conduct pacified the weavers, and they dispersed peaceably. A similar riot broke out in April, and the weavers again attacked the East India House. According to Salmon, " they had very near seized the treasure of the East India House."‡

In spite of all these, Parliament did not move again until 1700. Child died in 1699, and this greatly facilitated legislation against the Company's trade.

III

The Bill of 1699

After April, 1697, we cease to hear for some time " the groans of the poor weavers." The reason is rather obscure. However there is a significant statement in *England's Almanack* (1700)§ that after 1696 " English manufactures again flourished." Davenant also refers to a great call for woollen goods. At the same time there was a visible depression in the East India Company's imports and sales. What with the defiant attitude of the interlopers and the wasteful rivalries with the new corporation, the old Company was brought to dire straits; and even its very existence

---

* Foster, *East India House*, p. 72.

† Luttrel, IV; *Post Boy*, March 23; *The Flying Post*, M. 23 (Nichols Newspapers, Bodl.). See also Foster, p. 73.

‡ *Chronological History*, 1697, quoted in Smith's *Chronicon*, I, p. 404.

§ Works, Vol. I, p. 69.

was at stake. Yet with seeming calmness, they wrote to India in March, 1698, that they were " going to pursue trade with vigour in spite of the acts of Parliament,"* (i.e., establishing the new Company).

About 1698 the East India trade revived with redoubled vigour. Imports again mounted up to high figures. The old Company, the new Company, and the numerous inter- lopers plied their trade indefatigably, and the English market was flooded with their imports. Bullion worth a million and a half pounds was sent to India in the short period between Michælmas, 1698 and February, 1699 ; and yet there was other bullion exported during the same period from the Continent on account of English merchants. The total imports of Indian textiles during the years 1698 and 1699 beat all previous record. Consequently those subsidiary trades that arose to work up or deal in East India goods flourished beyond all measure. These tradesmen in their petitions before Parliament claimed to be "as numerous as the weavers," and really there is some justification for this boast. According to a petition † of 1700, about one thousand families were then engaged merely in retailing East India goods.

The weavers became again alarmed. Disaffection was rife in Spitalfields and in other silk and worsted centres. They raised their complaints once more by means of pamphlets and petitions. This was the opportunity for men like " Prince Butler " to give vent to their satirical outbursts. But the Ministry was not quite ready to give heed to their prayers. This was not due to any indifference, because the independent Whigs and Tories who had the majority in those days did not mind the king or the ministers ; nor were they specially concerned about the Company The hold of the Company on the Tory party was fast loosening ; and it was a Tory Parliament that inflicted the most crushing blow on the Company. However the ministry was interested in putting off the prohibition of Indian imports. Government wanted money very badly, and the free Indian merchants offered to advance £2,000,000 in lieu of a charter

---

* MS. Letter Books, Vol. IX.
† H. MSS. Comm., V, IV, p. 94.

to trade with India. Until this contract was completed, the ministry could not pay heed to the weavers. The promoters of the new Company also did various things to please the weavers.* They promised not to trade in Indian textiles and to do everything in their power to destroy that trade. They reached such a good understanding with the weavers that late in 1698 some of them dined at the Weavers' Hall, and as a result of their clever speeches the simple weavers promised to vote for two of the India merchants who were standing for Parliamentary elections. But not long afterwards the new Company also imported vast quantities of calicoes, and showed no special concern for English industries. The poor weavers became again desperate.

Parliament, however, did not delay the promised measures of redress. In the last month of 1699, there was a Committee† appointed by the House of Commons to consider means for "the better providing for the poor and letting them to work." The House had also reports from the Commissioners of Trade and Plantations condemning the importation of calicoes. ‡ Soon after the dawn of the new century (January 8, 1700) the House ordered the Committee to prepare a Bill for that purpose. Accordingly a Bill was introduced by Mr. Pelham on February 5, "for the more effectual employment of the poor and encouraging the Manufactures of England." The title is significant, as it studiously excludes all mention of calicoes and silks. Yet the body of the Bill was the same as that presented to the House in 1696 and 1697. Perhaps these tactics were calculated to defeat the opposition of the upper House. However there were important changes in the provisions of the Bill. The two most prominent ones were (i) the exclusion of calicoes painted or printed in England from the operation of the Act, and (ii) the introduction of the system of bonded ware-housing to serve as a means of carrying on trade without encouraging the consumption of the same

---

* *A True Relation* . . ., p. 2.
† Commons Journals, XIII, p. 97. See also pp. 176, 184, 188.
‡ Brit. Mus. MSS. 24 B. They sent a report also in 1697.

goods at home. The first provision saved the various subsidiary industries that subsisted on working up Indian calicoes, and as we shall see later laid the foundations of a flourishing calico-printing industry in England. The second also had momentous results on the navigation and shipping of England. The two important amendments made by the House of Lords in 1697 were completely ignored. French and other foreign silks were not prohibited, and wearing of prohibited goods was not brought under penalty.

The Bill had a rapid progress through both the Houses. On February 5, it was read for the first time. On the same day Godolphin presented before the House an account of the calicoes and silks imported and exported in 1698 and 1699. Two days later, the Bill was read a second time, and then it went to the Committee on which served Godolphin, Montague, and all members who represented the manufacturing counties of Norfolk, Wilts, Devon and Yorkshire. The linen drapers of London petitioned to be heard, but the prayer was refused. On February 9, the Committee made its report, with some amendments, and the Bill was passed. It is significant that immediately after this on the same day was taken up the Bill allowing the old Company to remain a corporation.

The House of Lords took up the Bill on February 13.* Immediately petitions came from the dealers in East India goods. Powys and Filmer represented the petitioners. The weavers too had their lawyers to argue for them. The petitioners were heard in Committee. John Berne, a retailer, said he had £2,500 worth of East India goods, and could not sell them out within the period specified in the Bill. However the Lords passed the Bill without much delay; nor did they make any amendments this time. On the day the Bill was entered in the statute book there were great rejoicings in all weaving centres.

The main provisions of the Statute may be briefly summarised. The preamble is very remarkable, as it contains the quintessence of the bullionist doctrine. It was stated that " the continuation of the trade to the East Indies in the

* H. MSS. Comm., Vol. IV, p. 93-94.

same manner and proportions as it hath been for two years last past must inevitably be to the great detriment of this kingdom by exhausting the treasure thereof and melting down the coin and taking away the labour of the people, whereby very many of the manufacturers of this nation have become excessively burdensome and chargeable to their respective parishes and others are thereby compelled to seek for employment in foreign parts." Therefore from September 29, 1701, " all manufactured silks, Bengalls, and stuffs mixed with silks or herba, of the manufacture of Persea, China or East Indies and all Calicoes painted, dyed, printed or stained there which are or shall be imported into this kingdom of England, dominion of Wales, and town of Berwick-on-Tweed shall not be worn or otherwise used within this kingdom." No other people were more pleased with this part of the Bill than the calico printers. It provided for their " plentiful increase " whilst the Bill of 1696 threatened to stifle their very existence. But this offered an occasion for future complaint.

The arrangements made for safeguarding trade while prohibiting the goods for home consumption were the most interesting of the whole statute. The prohibited goods were immediately on importation to be put into approved warehouses and were not to be taken out except for exportation, and not until sufficient security was given that every part of it would be exported and not landed again in any part of the kingdom. The securities would be discharged without any fee, upon certificate under seal of the chief magistrate in any place beyond the sea or two known English merchants that such goods were there landed, or upon proof of creditable persons that such goods were taken by enemies or perished in the seas. This provision served very well to encourage trade without introducing the goods into the country, and made for the growth of shipping. London became thereby a great warehouse for the store of goods destined for various parts of the world. Walpole and other financiers expanded the system later, and made various improvements in it. How was this system originally devised ? There is some reason to surmise that the French Arrét of 1686* gave the suggestion to the English legislators. It is significant that copies of the French law are found in the collection of papers belonging to the Commissioners of Trade and Plantations. Besides, its provisions are quoted by some of the pamphlets of the day. According to one of those pamphlets,† the bonded warehouse system was suggested in Parliament after the failure of the Bill of 1697 ; but it is not clear who suggested it.

Very severe penalties were imposed on the slightest violation of the law. All prohibited goods found in any place except in recognised warehouses were forfeit, and should be seized just like other uncustomed goods ; and such forfeited merchandise should be sold by the candle at the customs house to exporters giving security as above. A third of the price thus realised went to the king, and the rest to the person or persons who prosecuted. The offenders forfeited also £200, which should be divided likewise between the Crown and the prosecutor. Those who clandestinely imported prohibited goods were to forfeit £500 besides the goods imported. The penalties thus imposed were certainly very mild when compared to the French Arrét. According to the latter, salesmen of prohibited goods were to be fined 3,000 livres and were to be excluded for ever from all handicrafts and trades, and those who brought those goods in were to be condemned to the galleys for three years, and, if with armed force, for life. The fines were divided as in the English statute but the participants were to be the informer, the hospitals of the place of crime, and the revenue farmers; and the sum was to be equally divided between them.

The prohibited goods were to pay only a half subsidy on importation, and all other duties were abolished.‡ Thereby trade in them was otherwise encouraged, and the companies were partly propitiated. But this came into force only after September 29, 1701. Until then a temporary duty of fifteen per cent. *ad valorem* was put on all prohibited goods imported, and this was to be charged on the gross sales. Muslins

---

* *Arret du Conseil D'etat de Roy* . . . (1686). Copies found in the Public Record Office (Board of Trade Papers).
† *A True Relation* . . . (1699).
‡ 11 and 12 William and Mary, *c.* 10.

were not prohibited, but soon an import duty of fifteen per cent. was imposed on them. The French Arrét gave even greater concessions to the trade of their favourite India Company.

There were also numerous other provisions in the statute of 1700 concerning the warehousing and keeping of accounts ; and it also safeguarded the prosecutor from peril by imposing the *onus probandi* on the law-breakers, and making other provisions of a judicious nature.

The important item of muslins was excluded from the operation of the Bill as also plain calicoes of various kinds. Herein lies the greatest difference between the English and French statutes—a difference that is in itself a commentary on the different national characteristics of the two countries. The theoretically minded French, with their devotion to stern logic, not only prohibited all kinds of Indian textile goods (except the white calicoes and muslins sold by the one French Company), but even made stringent provision to suppress the calico-printing industry that had arisen in the country by punishing printers, mould-makers and others concerned in the industry. But the practical-minded English with their innate common sense prohibited only printed calicoes and allowed plain ones to be freely brought in and worked up in the country. The result of the two policies was that while France drove her ingenious artisans and craftsmen into other lands and thereby impoverished itself, England unconsciously laid the foundations of the calico-printing industry which first flourished for a long time in Surrey and later reached great prosperity in Lancashire.*

* The Act of 1700 has been much criticised by Free Trade theorists on the one hand, and by critics of Imperialism on the other. The contention of the former, that it was a mercantilist folly, is based upon a misconception of the objects of Protectionism and an underestimation of the results of Protectionist policy. The contention that the Act injured Indian industries is more serious, but we must remember in this connection, as Mr. William Foster points out (*East India House*, p. 78) that India was then an independent country and had none of the special claims which she to-day has on Great Britain. Nor is it correct to say that the Indian manufacturers were much harmed by the Act, for England was not the only or even the principal market then served by India. Dr. S. A. Khan (*East India Trade*, p. 291, and *passim*), shows by an elaborate reasoning, that the Act was passed by a Government dominated by the weavers, and that the " people " are to blame for the " follies of Government." His reasoning is by no means easy to follow, and leaves one in doubt as to what the main issues were.

Chapter VI

THE FORTUNES OF THE CALICO TRADE (1700–1719)

I

First Effects of Prohibition

THE results of the Act of 1700 have been variously estimated. Even on its immediate effects with which alone we are concerned in the present connection, there is by no means any agreement among contemporaries. *England's Almanac*, published immediately after the Bill passed, speaks of great rejoicings in several places. "A gentleman concerned in Trade" who publishes his impressions* on the Act in 1708, dwells at great length on "the most beneficial effect" of the Act, and tells how London, Canterbury and Norwich had rapidly come to a state of real prosperity within eighteen months after the Bill became law. "In London," he says, "the maker has a market for his goods and artists and workmen are returned from their places of dispersion." "The empty streets and houses are again inhabited." As for Canterbury, men who fled returned "in shoals and companies, and their homes and their bellies are full, and they rather want hands than work." According to him, the landowners also benefited by the rise in the price of wool and high rents everywhere.

A pamphlet of 1719 spoke of the "good results" after 1700, and that "the face of things changed and business and plenty succeeded."† These reports are also strengthened by various petitions in 1719. Canterbury silk weavers stated in their petition before the Commissioners of Trade and Plantations‡ that "this good Act" gave them "a new life."

---

* *Reflections on the Prohibition Act* (1708), Golds. Libr.
† *A Brief State of the Question* (1715), p. 13.
‡ Public Record Office. C.O. 388. Vol. XXI, p. 268.

THE FORTUNES OF THE CALICO TRADE (1700-1719)

This view, however, was not shared by all, and as early as 1702 there were many discontented parties among the weavers. Their cause of discontent was the very thing for which we might now congratulate the legislators. One George Morley petitioned to the Trade Commissioners* in 1702 that " the Act hath not had ye good effect which was expected thereby," and he even went to the length of saying that it was " much worser with (woollen) manufactory than ever." A petition to the House of Commons in 1703 from London complains that " the Act had not produced the desired effect."† The point of complaint was that it " hath rather occasioned the figuring printing and staining calicoes here in England to the discouragement of our woollen manufactures." White calicoes were allowed to be imported by the Act, and they could be sold even cheaper in England than before owing to the abolition of all previous duties except a half-subsidy. Even the additional duty of fifteen per cent. subsequently imposed on white calicoes did not discourage this trade to any great extent. Besides, the prohibited goods were soon sent in vast quantities into the Colonies and other places where formerly English woollens were being used. At home, however, there was a sudden popularity for English cloths and silks ; but this did not last very long.

The manufacturers soon found that their expectations were not fulfilled. In 1701 there must have been few printed calicoes to compete with English textiles, but after some time the market was flooded with cheap and beautiful calicoes and linens printed at home. There were also calicoes clandestinely imported from Holland, for the Act indirectly encouraged illegal trade. The Commissioners reported in 1702 that " the prohibiting of painted calicoes from India to be consumed in England has not had the desired success.‡

The East India Company was not so much humiliated

* C.O. 388, Vol. XXI.
† Commons Journals, Vol. XIV, January 12, 1703.
‡ Report on House of Lords MSS., 1702-04, p. 71. Quoted in Foster, *op. cit.*, p. 76.

by the Act as it might be supposed. As they wrote to India in 1700, they " could not imagine how such sumptuary laws could last long." For the time being they ordered their servants not to send the prohibited goods, but they had good prospects of trade owing to the low duty imposed on even prohibited goods, " by which means," they thought, " they could the better bear their lying in the warehouse for a markett." They regarded the prohibition as " no better than laying a tax on the nation by making goods 50 to 100 p.c. dearer " ; and they could not imagine the Parliament would long continue the prohibition. Even if it did, the directors were sure that foreign markets would find a sale for their goods.

Yet the Company was hard hit. There was a general fear in England that calicoes would not be worn any longer and drapers were reluctant to keep much stock. The Company had a succession of losing sales. " Soosays put up at 40s. and not half sold " . . . " the Choukaris put up at 18s would not sell," and similarly with Chana-churis, Cattanes, Ginghams and Chintzes. Complete accounts of these sales were sent to India in order to show what goods were wanted and at what prices. The lists of goods to be provided get very slender ; and the despatches get dry, short and uninteresting. " Send no more Chintz, and Calicoes," they wrote to Madras, " since the duty of 15 p.c. is too heavy." Similar instructions were sent to Bengal about muslins, and those were repeated for some time.

However, when some branches of the Company's business suffered, others flourished, and this made up for the loss to a certain extent. White Calicoes were much wanted in England for printing, and cotton yarn was sought by fustian makers and others. Hence the rapid rise of the imports of white calicoes, dimities and yarn. Madras had to send all the floretta yarn that could be got, and also all kinds of plain goods.* The plain calicoes of Anjengo were much in demand at this time.

Muslins had to pay an import duty of fifteen per cent. This discouraged plain muslins but acted as a preference

* Letter Books, X, No. 20, 1701.

for dearer varieties, for all kinds of muslins had to pay the same duty. The result was that there arose a growing demand for finer goods of various kinds. " Send finer Muslins," the Directors wrote to Bengal, because " they would bear the duty better." To Madras they wrote :— " Henceforward we care more for quality than quantity, send only good commodities . . . . cull the goods brought by natives."* Bengal was asked to send the finest muslins. Some goods went out of fashion (like quilts), but others came into vogue (e.g., Betellees). We will revert to the fortunes of the Company's trade in Chapter V.

II

Calico Printing in England†

It is now really difficult for us to realise that 200 years ago hardly any genuine cotton cloth was made in England. It is true that " cottons " were spoken of even in the sixteenth century ; and in the seventeenth we have definite records‡ mentioning the manufacture of cloth from cotton wool imported from the Levant, but these were not genuine cotton cloth but the hybrid fustians made of linen warp and cotton weft. English artisans did not know in those days how to make cotton strong enough to serve for warp. Successive attempts were made, as we shall see, but with little success till the inventions of Hargreaves and Arkwright. However, if genuine calicoes could not be made, yet the English artisan succeeded in starting what still remains an important branch of cotton industry—the printing of calicoes and other cotton cloth.

It was supposed, even by certain contemporary writers, that the calico-printing industry was started in England after the prohibition of calicoes in 1700. Thus Daniel Defoe wrote in 1717 :—" No sooner were the East India Chintzes and painted calicoes prohibited from abroad but some of

* L.B., XI, April 16, 1708.

† For a more detailed account, see the author's paper in the *Eng. Hist. Review*, April, 1924, *The Beginnings of Calico Printing in England*.

‡ Lewis Roberts, *The Treasure of Trafficke* (1641). W. H. Price traces it to the beginning of the century. *Quarterly Journal of Economics*, Vol. XX.

Britain's unnatural children . . . . set their arts to work to mimick the more ingenious Indians and to legitimate grievances by making it a manufacture." But this is a mistake. The industry existed before the Prohibition Act of 1700. It will be remembered that some of those who were engaged in this industry petitioned Parliament against the Bill of 1696. The industry was of earlier origin; yet it is true to say that it was after 1700 that it flourished and took firm root in the country. The Commissioners of Trade and Plantations brought out this change in their report of 1702.[*] " Though it was hoped," wrote they, " that this prohibition would have discouraged the consumption of these goods, we found that the allowing calicoes unstained to be brought in has occasioned such an increase of the printing and staining calicoes here and the printers and painters have brought that art to such perfection that it is more prejudicial to us than it was before the passing of the Act." A similar report was made by the Commissioners in 1707 also.[†]

According to the " judicious " Anderson, calico printing began in England in 1676 ; and this is confirmed by a patent to one William Sherwin in that year " for the invention of a new and speedy way for printing broadcloth which being the only true way of East India printing and stayning such kinds of goods." The same gentleman appeared before the House of Lords in 1696, and claimed that he printed calicoes and even woollen cloth[‡] ; but he admitted that it would not bear washing. Evidently he must have used pigments as they first did in France, and the madder and resist process of the Indians was not yet known in England.

In 1690, calico-printing was started in the Old Deer Park at Richmond, and a patent was given in that year to René Grillét for painting and printing calicoes. This was perhaps the first real calico printing factory in England. The owner was a Frenchman, and Baines[§] (followed by other

---

[*] Report of House of Lords, MSS., 1702-04, p. 71.
[†] Ditto, 1706-08, p. 250.
[‡] H. MSS. Com., II, No. 1050.
[§] Baines, *History of Cotton Manufacture in England* (1845), p. 259. Cunningham, *Growth of English Industry and Commerce* (Modern Times), 517. Baker, p. 46-47.

writers) surmises that he was a Huguenot refugee from France, but from the subsequent mention in various pamphlets that calico printing was done by French Roman Catholics,* it is likely that the Frenchman in question was a calico-printer forced to flee the country by the stringent arrét of 1686 rather than by religious persecution. We know that he was some time in Holland before he came over to England, and it is certain that he perfected his art there under the care of the clever Dutch master printers. His factory stood about 150 feet from the Thames, and it would appear that a large number of people, both men and women, were employed there. According to local records, Richmond was overrun by these calico-printers, who were " a saucy and independent lot." † They were mostly Frenchmen and Roman Catholics. They were hated on both accounts, and perhaps it was this that made the legislature not very anxious about their welfare.

Soon another factory arose at Bromley Hall, in Essex. A grant was made to Francis Pousset in 1694 for a " new way of preparing crape in flowers, ramages, etc." The factory of Bromley Hall stood number 1 in the Excise Books when the first duty was imposed on calico printing (1712), and certainly it must have been the most important factory at that time. Other factories soon arose in Lewisham, Mitcham, Wandsworth and other places around London.

These factories were engaged in working up the plain calicoes, imported from India for the English market, by dyeing, printing, painting, staining and other processes. The methods employed were copied from India, where they had been practised from time immemorial. Wooden blocks, were used for printing—blocks of sycamore, about five to ten inches square. The method of printing employed was an adaptation of the Indian madder and resist process, which is first mentioned in the grant of 1694. Later, copper-plates were used, instead of wood. These early methods are exhibited in the Victoria and Albert Museum at South

---

* Public Record Office, C.O., 389, p. 309 ; Trade Commr's Report ; also Weavers' True Case, p. 23.

† Richard Crisp, *Richmond and its Inhabitants* (1866) p. 115.

Kensington, and were first explained to Europe in 1742 by a Jesuit missionary, Pére Courdoux* (who, by the way, deserves to be better known as the first to suggest the hypothesis of an Indo-European race).† The special process called Turkey red, introduced to France by an Armenian, was made of Chaya root and Kasha leaves. It baffled chemists until it was cleared up in 1902 by a calico printer at Leyden, Felix Dreissen, who got the secret from a native dyer in Madura (South India).

The Dutch were the first to adopt these Indian processes in Europe. From them, the French and the English got the secret. The first great French calico printers,‡ Daniel Vasserot and his nephew Antoine Fazy, learned the art from Holland, and after the industry was prohibited in France they practised it at Geneva. The calicoes printed in Europe in those days were sold under the pretence that they were made in India.§ Such an assurance was the only way of satisfying the ladies that the quality was good.

We can from extant records form an idea of the employees in a calico printing factory in those days.‖ The principal workmen were drawers, cutters, printers, job-printers, grounders, tearers and fieldmen. The *drawers* invented patterns, or copied them from the Indian chintzes ; for the designs on the English-printed calicoes were almost the same as those on the India-printed. The tree of life, the peacocks, the snakes, the bamboos—all were evidently adaptations of Masulipatam work. The *cutters* engraved these designs on wood, for the use of the printer. *Printers* made the first impressions of any colour on calicoes. *Job-printers* printed old calicoes and linens ; their work is said to have given " great encouragement to servants to rob their masters or mistresses, for by getting it printed alters it so much as cannot be known." *Grounders*, mostly women, put the finishing colours. The *tearers* were boys and girls

* *Recueil des Lettres Edifiantes et curieuses*, Vol. XXVI.

† Max Muller, *Lectures on the Origin of Language*, Vol. I.

‡ *Nos Anciens et Leurs Oeuvres*, 1906, pp. 103-118.

§ Connoiseur, 1917. The English printed calicoes were called *Londrindiana*. This name tells its own tale.

‖ Public Record Office, C.O. 388, Vol. XXI p. 223.

that attended the printers when at work. *Fieldmen* were those who whitened the calicoes and were ordinary unskilled day-labourers. Only the first three classes seem to have had any sort of training. All these employees worked only eight or ten months in the year.

After the Prohibition Act of 1700, the printing industry flourished* more than ever. The woollen and silk manufacturers soon realised that the victory that they thought they gained in 1700 was in reality a defeat. John Haynes wrote in 1706 that "greater quantities of Calicoes had been printed and worn in England annually since the importing of it was prohibited than ever was brought from India."† The rapid growth of the industry is also evident from the sudden demand that set in in England for plain calicoes. This can be very well studied in the Directors' despatches‡ after 1702. In 1704-5 as many as 965,009 calicoes were imported, which was above the figures for most years before 1700. In 1703, hardly two years after the statute came into force, the woollen and silk manufacturers of London, Norwich, Linton and other centres, petitioned Parliament against the increased consumption of calicoes.§ A Committee sat on the matter and a bill was soon passed to impose a duty of fifteen per cent. *ad valorem* on the plain calicoes imported from India, and thus put them on the same footing as muslins. However a full drawback was allowed on re-exportation. We do not know exactly how it affected the new industry. As Chalmers‖ pointed out, the duty must have been rather light considering the fact that the prime cost of calicoes was only a fraction of the value after being printed. However the printers complained in 1711 that the fifteen per cent. duty reduced their industry to a third of its previous strength.**

The weavers still looked upon their young rival with a jealous eye. They wanted to suppress it altogether and

* Espinasse, *Lancashire Worthies*, p. 297.
† Golds. Libr. *View of the Present State of Clothing Trade*, p. 19.
‡ MS. Letter Books, Vol. XI, XII, and XIII.
§ *Commons Journals*, Vol. XIV, Jan. and Feb. 1703.
‖ Public Record Office, C.O. 390, Vol. XIV.
** Bromley Papers, Vol. II, 113, 134.

considered this the true national interest. And fortunately for them, Government in those days looked at the question from the same standpoint. To satisfy the clamorous weavers —and partly also to find money for war—an excise duty was imposed on printed calicoes and linens.* Calico was charged 3d. a square yard, and linens 1½d. Calicoes and linens printed in one colour only were, however, exempted from the tax. Calico-printers and Scotch linen-makers furiously resisted the imposition and pointed out that it would ruin many people not only in Scotland, but in the north and north-west of England.† But their claims were not only disregarded, but the excise duty was raised two years later to 6d. and 3d. respectively on calico and linen. The printers proved that calicoes were already taxed to the amount of £46 10s. per cent. *ad valorem*, including the subsidy, the additional duty and 3d. excise duty ; and that the proposed duty would raise it to £82 10s. per cent.‡ This would, they urged, not only ruin the printing trade, but also favour the clandestine importation of Dutch printed calicoes, which were cheaper by one-half. But all this reasoning did not prevail against the avowed Colbertism of Parliament. The one staple industry of the country must be fostered at any cost.

In spite of this step-motherly policy of the State, the infant industry grew in vigour and importance. In 1711, the directors of the Company wrote to India : " Our people here will do it (i.e., printing) at one-half the price, and better colours and patterns." There was a demand from the Colonies and elsewhere for their goods and the industry expanded to meet the demand. In 1719§ there were many factories in the counties of London, Surrey, Kent and Essex. The chief entrepreneurs were Mauvillon, Watson, Haultain, Madam Bull, Quard and Gouyne. Mauvillon was a prominent calico printer in 1697, when he appeared before the House of Commons. He had in 1719 a workshop at Mitcham (Surrey)

* 10 Anne, C. 19.
† Bromley Papers, Vol. II, No. 137.
‡ *Op. cit.*, Vol. IV, No. 29.
§ Public Record Office, C.O. 389, Vol. XXVII, p. 223.

and another at Wandsworth. Watson had three, which were located at Morisses Cassau, Bunhill Fields and Wandsworth. Most of the establishments were hard by the banks of the Thames.

Like other industries introduced by foreigners* in that period, calico-printing was organised on a capitalist basis. It had no guild traditions to keep up ; nor was it possible for it to become a domestic industry like the woollen. The various processes had to be carried on in conjunction and artisans had to work in some common place in order to co-operate effectively. Besides the employers were calculating capitalists, seeking a profitable investment for their money. As Cunningham has shown, capital is bound to be " an important factor in the transferring of a trade to a new area." All these circumstances combined to make calico-printing a factory industry of the modern type. The factories seem to have been fairly well-equipped, and were located within convenient reach of water. In 1720, they claimed before the Trade Commissioners that they had fitted up a costly equipment by " erecting workhouses, preparing ground, conveying water and providing costly utensils," and that the whole plant would go to rack and ruin if calicoes were prohibited. It is also interesting to note that large numbers were employed in each factory. Mauvillon had 152 workmen in a single factory, of whom sixty were fieldmen, forty tearers, twelve grounders, twenty-eight printers and twelve drawers and cutters. Watson's factories were smaller ; yet in one of them he employed as many as seventy-seven labourers. Not only grown up men but women and children were employed in these factories.

The woollen and silk weavers emphatically denied that calico printing was a manufacture, but the printers affirmed it with equal vehemence. The latter claimed, and with some justification, that they put more additional value on calicoes than silk weavers did on raw silk, and yet silk was as much a foreign commodity as their calico. The printers hoped that their industry would " make a great

* Cunningham, *Growth of English Industry and Commerce* (Modern Times), p. 518.

addition to the trade of the nation, not only by advantageously employing many thousands of the poor, but by supplying the nation with a cheap commodity for home consumption."*

III

Beginnings of Cotton Manufacture

Various attempts were made during that period to make genuine cotton cloth in England. Cotton wool came from the Levant and the American colonies, but none could make a warp strong enough to weave cloth. In 1691, however, Mr. Barkstead, in a petition to Parliament, stated that he invented a method " of making callicoes, muslins and other fine cloth of that sort out of the cotton wool of the growth and produce of the Plantations, and the West Indies to a great perfection as those which are brought over and imported from Calicut and other places in the East Indies." A Bill was soon prepared and he was apparently given the patent he applied for. He soon petitioned that himself and a few others may be incorporated into a Company for the above purpose with the Earl of Nottingham as the first Governor. But nothing came out of the scheme.

It is, however, certain that some kind of cotton cloth was made in England about the year 1700, for we get faint glimpses of it in pamphlets and petitions of the period. As early as 1695, the Bristol Merchant, John Cary, wrote† that cotton wool had "become a great employment of the poor" and that it was made into dimities, tapes, stockings, gloves, besides several things wove fit as petticoats, waist-coats, drawers of different fancies and stripes. He even thought that "English workmen would exceed the East Indies for callicoes had they encouragement." In 1699, the same author was even more hopeful of the prospects of a cotton industry in England. " If the manufacture of wool will not please," he asks, "why may not one of cotton ? The

---

* Brit. Mus. 816, m. 14, No. 102.
† *Essay on Our Trade* (1695), p. 15.

primum of which the callicoes are made whereby we have great quantities imported every year from our own plantations in America." If encouragement were given, he (Cary) was sure that the finest thread could be spun in England, either in cotton or in wool. " We might, in time," he concludes, " make calicoes equal in their sorts with those imported from India and afford them as cheap as the Company now sells them, enough not only for our home expense, but also for exportation."*

Nor is Cary unsupported by other contemporary writings. A manuscript of 1706, preserved in the Goldsmiths' collection contains the following : " The imported manufactures of greater value do us mere mischief. Had we cotton enough, we can spin and weave it and make as good muslane as any the Indys afford, and *some of our weavers have actually done it*, whereof the Companies are too well aware to furnish us with over much " (italics mine).†

We get also faint echoes of such an industry in some petitions during the calico controversy of 1719-20. In a petition from Weymouth and Melcomb Regis sent by " the merchants, masters of ships, master workers, weavers and spinners of cotton wool imported from British Plantations and manufactured in the said town," as also by the Mayor, Aldermen, etc., of the Borough, it is stated that for many years past a manufacture had been carried on . . . for making cotton imported from the British plantations into cloth of diverse kinds, more particularly into such fabrics as imitate calicoes." The petition was made against the bill prohibiting calicoes, then pending before the House. It was read, but a motion to refer it to the whole House was lost by 190 votes to 68.

It is not easy to decide what credit should be given to the above account. The records available do not fully support the contention of the petition. Dorset was never an industrial county. It is true it had a hemp industry of

---

* *Discourse concerning the East India Trade, showing how it is unprofitable to the Kingdom of England* (1699), p. 7.

† *The Meanes of a Most Ample Increase of the Wealth and Strength of England in a Few Years* (1706, MSS.), fol. 50.

some importance, and it depended upon foreign trade for its raw materials.* Coker, in 1732, writes of sailcloth being made in Dorset. Cotton often accompanied linen, and this was possibly the case at Dorset. It is also known that imported cotton yarn was used in the manufacture of stockings, especially at Abbotsbury.† It is likely that some of the cotton yarn imported was used to make cloth. It is also significant that the chief petitioners were merchants and masters of ships, who were probably afraid that the use of their cotton yarn imports would be entirely stopped in England. We have unfortunately no further evidences about this early venture in cotton manufacturing.

In 1719 the calico printers represented to the Trade Commissioners that the calicoes they printed " were made here of cotton imported from our Plantations." Mr. Asgill stated the same in his pamphlet. It is, however, certain that the bulk of the calicoes they printed were made in India. A few may have been made in England, but we have no definite records to prove it. Yet the statements of adversaries definitely point to the existence of calico-making in England. For example, when Claudius Rey‡ answered Asgill's statement just noted, he did not deny it completely but only said : " There never was in the whole kingdom ten looms of these callicoes, and these so very coarse that when printed they are not sold above two shillings and 4d. per yard." This statement is unmistakable evidence of the beginnings of a cotton industry. However, owing to obvious technical difficulties this did not become important until the inventions of Hargreaves and Arkwright.

When the controversy on calicoes was raging in the country, some enthusiastic schemes were adumbrated, two of which are particularly noteworthy. One§ was " a proposal by several ladies and others to make, print, and stain callicoes in England " and the subscribers to it were to be women dressed in calico. This scheme was certainly the result of

---

* Victoria County History : Dorset, Vol. II, p. 348.
† Cooke, Topogr. Dorset, p. 62, quoted in *op. cit.*
‡ Observations on Asgill's Brief Answer (1719).
§ State Petitions, Domestic, Petition Entry Book III, p. 450.

the spleen excited among women by the weavers' insults. The other scheme was a more serious and practicable one. In November, 1719, when the Trade Commissioners were concerting measures for redressing the grievances of the weavers, Richard Wrightson, Oliver Hurst and other linen drapers laid before them a splendid scheme for establishing a calico manufacture in England, whereby they hoped they would be able " to transplant a very considerable branch of the treasure of the Indies and make an addition to our trade." They hoped also thereby to solve the question of unemployment and the rivalry between calico printers and weavers. Soon afterwards they petitioned to be incorporated into a company by royal charter. They calculated that 1,627 tons of cotton wool would be necessary to make calicoes enough for England, and that this would employ 38,160 people. Government, too, would gain a great deal by the excise duty on printing, and could raise a large loan on the security of this annual revenue. The scheme was admirable, but it did not materialise. Had this fructified, there would have arisen a nascent cotton industry on capitalist lines.

After 1720 it was illegal to wear cotton cloth and therefore a regular industry was out of the question. Manchester went on making fustians, but it had to wait long to become " That city of cotton twists and twills."*

IV

" But in country or town
Now no lass will go down
But a tawdry callico madam."†

The Act of 1700 had left a loophole for those who were keen on wearing calicoes and chintzes. While prohibiting their importation, it tacitly allowed their use, provided they were worked up at home. Had the Lords' amendment of 1697 been accepted by the Commons, things would have

* Calico Printer's Clerk (a ballad).
† Spitalfields Ballad, 1719.

been far otherwise. Still, the women were for some time afraid to appear in prohibited clothing, but soon they flung their fears to the winds and went back to their old ways. Calico and chintz continued to be the fashion among all classes of people " as well in the country as in the city." The pamphlets that appeared not long after the Prohibition Act noted this and complained that more calicoes were being worn than before. From 1707, when " J.B." ridiculed the " lite women wearing lite commodities," to 1720 when that master of sarcasm, Daniel Defoe, emptied the vials of his vitriolic satire upon women for " their passion for their fashions," we can trace the growth and shiftings of the use of these " printed tandrums and the gewgaws of the East Indies."

The writers and petitioners of 1719 certainly stated their case too strongly on both sides. The Canterbury Weavers complained* that " little else was seen among the common people . . . but callicoes, and amongst the gentry but prohibited chintz." " Don't we see," wrote one memorialist, " the ladies and all their sex dressed in their calicoes and linnens ; and not only dressed but also a stock of different garments by them ready made up . . . of which any one may be convinced that is the least acquainted in families."† This is repeated in the innumerable petitions that came before the Trade Commissioners and the House of Commons in 1719 and 1720.

Granting these were interested reports, this could not be said of Defoe, who, whatever his faults, was not in the weavers' employ. " All the poor sort of people," he wrote, " especially country people and servants, most of the middling tradesmen's families, in a word almost all women that cannot afford to wear silks, now clothe themselves and their children in calicoes or printed linnen ; and not only these but a great many of the gentry and better sort of people also."

In arriving at a reasonable conclusion on this question, we must distinguish the different social classes and the sort

* Public Records Office, C.O. 388, Vol. XXVII, p. 216.
† *Ibid*, p. 247.

of dress that each class used to wear. There were (1) the women of the gentry, who formerly used brocades and venetians; (2) the tradesmen's wives, who wore silk damasks; (3) country farmers' wives and other "good country dames," who appeared usually in worsted damasks, flowered russets, calimancoes and so forth. The weavers' advocates* pointed out that the first class had come to wear "outlaw'd Indian chintz," the second English and Dutch printed calicoes, and the third class used almost solely ordinary calicoes and printed linen. Thereby it was asserted that English manufactures were largely displaced. Their opponents did not completely deny it, but maintained that they overstated the case. The higher classes used chintz and calico only for variety and still bought the old stuffs as before, and the poorer classes could not afford to buy good calicoes as they had become dear—even dearer than wool—owing to the heavy duties.

The higher classes did certainly go in for cotton clothing even after 1700, but the calicoes printed in Holland and England, were considered too vulgar for them. They showed still a passion for the muslins and chintzes that came direct from India. Chintz was but calico printed in India. but it was regarded as specially graceful for smart gowns. However it is easy to exaggerate the consumption of Indian goods among the gentle-born. George Chalmers, a keen observer of his time, has given us sufficient hints for guarding ourselves against over-statement. Before 1700, he says most ladies used muslin nightrails, made and received visits in muslin aprons, and both gentlemen and ladies used muslin ruffles. But after 1700, nightrails were "entirely disus'd" and visits were usually made in short silk aprons, and ruffles came to be made of cambric or fine lawn. Gentlemen who formerly used muslin neckcloths (Steenkirks) began to appear in turn-overs. Certainly chintz gowns were still used for variety, but Chalmers would put it at a tenth of the quantity used in 1699.

The lower classes at the same time increased their consumption of cotton goods, but chiefly those printed in

* Rey, *Weavers' True Case* (1719).

England and Holland. Even Chalmers admits this. Any one who passed through the streets with eyes open could always meet " Calico-madams " everywhere.* " Scarce any chambermaid was without a calico-gown." It was very decent and yet cheap, and could be washed. Especially between 1717 and 1719, the use of calicoes became very common. Calico gowns were usually lined with silk before, but from about 1717, calico itself was used for linings too.† Children were mostly clothed in calicoes and linen, and little of " Tammis " was used for their dress.

" Let anyone but cast their eyes," wrote Defoe, " among the meaner sort playing in the streets, or of the better sort at boarding schools and in our families ; the truth is too plain to be denied."

At the same time the use of calicoes and chintz served the purpose better than other stuffs. And the *Manufacturer‡* spoke the truth when it wrote, " As the streets are crowded with calico madams, the houses are stuff'd with calico furniture."

The literature of the period abounds in the most satirical attacks upon the new fangled fashions of women. Their " butterfly gowns " and " thin painted old sheets "§ were held up to ridicule in many a witty ballad and poem. A satirist wrote that women dressed in calico were " more like the Merry Andrews of *Bartholomew Fair* than like the ladies and the wives of a trading people."‖ Calico was called a " plague," " a tawdry, pie-spotted, flabby, ragged, low prized thing," . . . " a foreigner by birth, made the Lord knows where by a parcel of heathens and pagans that worship the devil and work for a half-penny a day."** A more philosophic writer considered calico a great scourge to Europe and expressed himself in sonorous words : " Europe like a body in warm bath with its veins opened lies bleeding to

---

* *The Interest of England* . . ., p. 7.
† *Weavers' True Case*, p. 9.
‡ Dec. 15, 1719 (Nichols Newspapers), *Bodleian.*
§ *Spitalfields Ballad* (1720). (Brit. Mus.)
‖ *Brief State of the Question* . . . (1720), p. 11.
** Golds. Libr., *The Female Manufacturers' Complaint.*

death and her bullion which is the life-blood of trade, flows to India. . . ."* " to enrich the Great Moghul's Subjects."

V

Growth of Smuggling

Evidently all the cotton goods then used in England were not printed and worked up there. Many of them came from India and from Holland. And since printed calicoes and chintzes could not be legally imported into the country, they must have come by illegal trade.

That there was smuggling going on at the time is certain, but the extent of it has been exaggerated. Peter Lekeux, of Spitalfields, in his statement before the Commissioners, of Trade and Plantations, maintained that "there were more calicoes worn in England that pay no duty than what are printed and worn here that do pay a duty, which may appear if we consider the great quantity of chintz that are worn by most ladies." David Clayton,† in 1719, noted the difference of prices of calicoes in London and the coast counties and found that retail prices in Norfolk, Essex and Kent were lower than even the wholesale prices in the city. Mr. Badcock and other London mercers stated before the Commissioners that " great quantities of foreign patterns were brought to their ships to match for linings."‡ In 1719 William Channiers of Dorchester, is reported to have seen £6,000 worth of calicoes being sold in a vessel, pretended to be Dutch, but with English masters." " The ship was like a faire," he wrote to a relative, " all ready money ; this is the trade that is drove."§ Finally we have the assertion of Defoe in *Mist's Journal*, that a prodigious quantity of foreign calicoes was run upon the shores by trading people.||

* *The Trade to India critically and calmly considered* (1720), p. 37.
† *System of Trade*, p. 10.
‡ Public Record Office, C.O. 388, o. 20.
§ Public Record Office, C.O. 388, Vol. XXVII, p. 214.
|| Lee, *Works of Daniel Defoe*, Vol. II, p. 139.

Now, what was the extent of smuggling ? The Commissioners of Trade had the best materials to judge on the question ; yet they did not utilise them scientifically. They made a rather feeble attempt to judge the quantities smuggled from certain assumed figures. For example, they took for granted that a million people in the country wore printed calicoes and linens at the rate of five yards per head per annum, and of this three-fourths were put down as calicoes. The import figures and those of the Excise Office did not tally with the above curious calculation, and by this method they concluded that over a million yards of calicoes were smuggled annually. Evidently it is puerile to depend on such guess-work. Nor have we now the means wherewith to arrive at exact figures.

On the other hand, Chalmers makes too little of the smuggling trade. Some of his reasons are very flimsy ; for instance, he says that he could not believe that " the buyers at East India sales who are gentlemen would demean themselves to deal in clandestine importation of muslins." However, in spite of his too great confidence in the honesty of gentlemen, he allowed that about 2,000 chintz were being smuggled annually for the wear " of persons of condition." These were bought at £4 in Holland and were sold at £7 or £8 here. Little muslin was smuggled according to him, because the duty was not too prohibitive. He would not put smuggled imports above £100,000.

How was this smuggling carried on ? It was believed at the time that part of the goods was run on shore from Holland, and that the East India Company smuggled in part of the goods re-exported. It was also thought that vast quantities of calicoes printed in England were entered for shipping, and got the stamp, and were then relanded and sold here. As "a citizen" wrote in 1720, " England being an Island there are a thousand places for putting goods on shore."* Once in England, the goods were " sold by pedlars and hawkers that go to people's houses to sell them, in prejudice of shopkeepers and fair traders."†

* *The Interest of England considered*, p. 229.
† Lekeux's Letter, Public Record Office, C.O. 389, Vol. XXVII, p. 292.

THE FORTUNES OF THE CALICO TRADE (1700-1719)

It is difficult to know accurately what part the Company had in this dishonourable trade. It is likely that some of the prohibited goods ordered by the court of directors from India were for smuggling. Indian chintzes were much valued, especially when they became rare, and women would pay any price for them. The interlopers and the Company's servants must have taken an active part in smuggling. In 1716 a bill was passed against the clandestine running of uncustomed goods, and many prosecutions were made according to this act. Early the next year, a parcel of unstamped muslins and other goods appraized at £641 16s. were found on board an East India ship after she was cleared. A similar parcel was subsequently seized from another ship. However it is difficult to believe that the general joint-stock had anything to do with this smuggling trade, and the Company cannot be taken to task for the misbehaviour of its servants. The Directors in their letter to the Trade Commissioners* pointed out that the smuggling that was going on was as much to their detriment as to that of the manufacturers and expressed their interest in suppressing illegal trade. However, pamphleteers persisted in laying questionable dealings at the door of the Company.

* Op. cit., p. 21. Memorial submitted by the Custom House solicitor.

CHAPTER VII

HOW PROTECTIONISM FINALLY TRIUMPHED

I

Introductory

IMMEDIATELY after Protectionism was set up as the foundation of English economic policy, the inevitable evils of such a system also made their appearance. As Dr. Cunningham has shown, State interference in commerce and industry, while benefiting some industries, was bound to become deleterious to others, especially when it was exercised by a Parliament ill-fitted for that purpose. How the interests of the various classes conflict in specific cases of protective legislation was adequately brought out by the calico controversy of 1696-1700. The Act of 1700 undoubtedly harmed numerous small industries ; yet everything was subordinated to the interest of the woollen industry, which was then universally regarded as the palladium of English prosperity. The victory thus gained, although far from complete, increased the confidence of the English weavers, and indirectly assured them that their clamours would be heeded, at least when they were sufficiently violent. To their great discomfort, they found that the new industry of calico-printing had prospered since the prohibition even more than their own manufactures, and their whole attention was concentrated upon the stifling of this infant industry. They had undoubtedly a right to be heard by the country when they complained of the havoc committed on home industries by foreign manufactures ; this was just and proper for patriots and parliaments. But when the manufacturers inveighed in 1719 against calico-printing, they could not have expected an equally favourable hearing, for that was also an English industry and employed numerous workers. Nevertheless, their clamours were successful, and in 1720, not only the importation but the consumption of cotton clothing in England was absolutely prohibited by Parliamentary statute, and for half a century this remained the law of the land. Protectionism received another triumph and even a more complete one. This marks the culmination of that system, which although successfully assailed by Adam Smith, was finally swept away only towards the middle of the nineteenth century.

However, the victory of the weavers was not so easily gained. A very protracted struggle preceded the Act of 1720. They had to try all the resources of their armoury before they could convince their legislators that they had a real grievance. First they resorted to rioting and other illegal methods, and their violence made the lot of calico-wearers insufferable. Then, taking to more reasonable methods, they carried on a sensational controversy through newspapers and pamphlets, and pestered the authorities with petitions and deputations. And when finally their object was attained, they gloried in " the felicity of being born Britons and of living in a nation and under a constitution where the cry of the poor will be heard against the clamour of the rich, against the assurance of the assured. . . ."*

Yet this struggle has none of the scientific interest that attaches to the controversy of 1696-1700. Numerous bulky pamphlets were published, but they merely repeated the stale arguments of the earlier writers. Indeed protectionism was ably stated by many writers, but on the free trade side nothing first-rate appeared this time. *The Advantages of the East India Trade Considered* was, indeed, an excellent publication, but this was only a reprint of the *Considerations*, published in 1701. Mr. Asgill, the Company's supporter in 1719-20, was a feeble writer, who could not even properly re-edit the arguments of Child and Davenant.

The nature of the protective legislation of 1720 has been much misunderstood. Even such an authoritative work as

* *The Manufacturer* February 17, 1920 (Bodleian).

the *Imperial Gazetteer of India* has the following erroneous statement on it* : " Cotton weaving was only introduced into England in the seventeenth century, and in 1721 an Act was passed prohibiting *in the interests of Manchester* the importation of printed calicoes from India " (italics mine). The sentence is a tissue of errors and inaccuracies. The clause about Manchester itself is doubly erroneous. It assumes wrongly that the Act was passed in the interests of the English cotton industry, and that Manchester was then the centre of that industry. But it will be evident as we proceed that the Act was passed in the interests of the woollen and silk manufacturers who were aggrieved by the use of cotton goods in England, and it did not matter in the least where these goods were made. As has been shown already, English weavers could not then make genuine cotton goods, and if some weavers succeeded it was not in Manchester but in Dorset or somewhere in the south. Manchester was not therefore interested in the controversy, and did not send up any petition. The Act was chiefly aimed against the calico-printers of Surrey and elsewhere (as also against East India merchants) and they naturally raised an outcry against it.

In view of the general misunderstanding about the controversy of 1719-20, it is proposed to deal with the various stages of it here in some detail.

II

The Weavers' Riots

The 10th of June was the Stuart Pretender's birthday, and ardent Jacobites celebrated it, even in 1719, with all the éclat possible in the privacy of their own houses. Towards the evening of that day, the vigilant Whigs noted some disaffection among the weavers in Spitalfields, who were seen to gather together and " murmur among themselves of the ruin of their trade owing to the consumption of Calicoes."† The next morning the peaceable citizens of London were roused from their slumbers by the rude shouts of mutinous

---

* Vol. III, p. 195.
† Boyer, *Political State of Great Britain*, Vol. XVII, p. 627.

weavers, who had come from Spitalfields. There were as many as 2,000 of them—" a mixed rabble of weavers, pickpockets, housebreakers, scoundrel Papists and Jacobites."[*] They assembled in several companies and went about the streets tearing calicoes off the women's backs and throwing *aqua fortis* on their clothes. The city authorities were informed and the Lord Mayor ordered the city gates to be closed. A troop of Horse Grenadier Guards were sent to Spitalfields to scare off the weavers. Two of the latter who resisted the guards had their heads cut off. Meantime a party of weavers had proceeded to Lewisham to destroy the calico-presses there, but the guards overtook them, and some of the insolent fellows were taken under custody. A few of them were carried before the Justice of the Peace, but he merely dismissed them with a reprimand, either " through fear of having his house pulled down or not apprehending the ill-consequences of his lenity."[†]

The weavers were by no means quieted. On the 12th they went about the city in small parties singing riotous ballads, and ill-treated all the women who appeared in printed calico or linen. Some women " were frighted into fits and others to miscarriage."[‡] Some of the rioters were seized and taken to the Tower, by order of the Governor, Colonel D'Oyley. The next day, when the guards had returned to Whitehall, weavers again came together to molest calico-wearers. The guards once more arrived and arrested some of them. The weavers attempted to rescue their fellows. Upon this, the trained bands fired at them with powder. The weavers were still insolent, and balls were fired, by which three persons were dangerously wounded. Two more were arrested for felony in tearing the gown of one Mrs. Becket.[§]

The weavers' rising created some sensation in the city, because it was associated with the cause of the Pretender. The newspapers reflect the prevalent fears among the people.

[*] *Weekly Journal or British Gazetteer*, June 13.
[†] Boyer, op. cit. p. 627.
[‡] *Weekly Journal or Saturday Post*, June 20.
[§] *Old Weekly Journal*, June 20.

John Humphreys, of St. Sepulchres, one of the ringleaders of the rising was a rabid Jacobite agitator, and had been already punished for sedition against King George. It was rumoured that his mother was a Roman Catholic, and this was quite enough to alarm London people at a time when the memories of the " Popish Plot " were still fresh in their minds. Under such circumstances he was immediately brought to trial and many witnesses deposed against him. William Baron and Richard Aaron had seen Humphreys drinking the Pretender's health, calling him King James III. Others had seen him distributing about £5 among the rabble for encouraging them to commit violence. After a short trial, Humphreys was indicted, together with his accomplices Baines, Picket, Hardy and Child. Humphreys had to stand twice in the pillory and suffer twelve months' imprisonment ; the others were punished less heavily.

The Master Weavers were afraid that they would be implicated in sedition and they dissociated themselves from the risings of their underlings. On July 1st, they wrote a letter of advice to their journeymen, in which while recognising the evil of calicoes, they reprimanded them for their violent methods on the ground especially that there were some likely to take advantage of their follies and endeavour to represent them as persons disaffected and thereby deprive them of the favour of Government. The journeymen in their reply promised to do according to the advice offered.

Already the newspapers had begun to take sides in the controversy. The Whig papers turned against the weavers, and this showed how superficial was the Whig attachment to Protectionism. This was the policy especially of the *Weekly Journal or British Gazetteer*. The Tory papers, naturally, took up the opposite side. Daniel Defoe was undoubtedly one of the leading journalists of the time. He then edited *The Weekly Journal or Saturday Post*, usually called *Mist's Journal*, which was first started for the Pretender's interest in 1716. Ever since Defoe became connected with that journal (in 1717) he wrote every week an introductory article commenting upon the chief events of the past week ;

and this is supposed to be the parent of the modern editorial or leading article.*

Defoe himself did not take up a consistent defence of the weavers. Now he wrote for the " poor " weavers, and now against the " riotous " weavers. On one occasion he ridiculed the women for their passion for calicoes ; and on another he sympathised with them for the insults they suffered. These were days when public men, not to speak of journalists, cared little for consistency. However the apparently paradoxical position of Defoe could perhaps be explained by his perception of both sides of the question. He knew the weavers' sufferings and recognised the justice of their complaints, but he did not like their unlawful methods and hated their unchivalrous treatment of women. As soon as the riots broke out, he wrote that their complaints, though just, were made " in an unpeaceable manner, and at an unseasonable time " (as Parliament was not then in session). He advised them to more lawful and moderate measures. However he conceded very much when he wrote that " it was absurd to dictate patience and forbearance to those in their condition without relieving them."†

The opposite side was taken by the *Weekly Journal or British Gazetteer* (very confusing indeed were the titles even of newspapers in those days !) It took its stand upon British liberty : " What signifies our riches," it asked, " and that liberty and property which we justly boast of except we have the liberty of eating and drinking or wearing these things when we have earned them ? " This newspaper emphatically denied that the calicoes were the cause of the miseries of tradesmen.

At the same time commenced a pamphlet controversy which was most acrimoniously kept up on both sides. Soon after the riots broke out, there appeared a provocative pamphlet, *The Weavers' Pretences Examined*, which condemned the Spitalfield Weavers' " murmurings in corners and

* Lee, *Works of Daniel Defoe*, Vol. I, 271-73.
† Lee, *op. cit.*, II, p. 136. *Weekly Journal or Saturday Post*, August 8.

riotous actions in open streets " and in the strain of Child, denied the right of one trade to complain of the prosperity of another. It was signed by " a merchant," and this called forth from the wise author of the *Chronicon Rusticum Commerciale* the remark that of all the pamphlets he had examined those " are the most replete with absurdities " which hid their authors' name under the pseudonym of " Merchant."* This attack brought out three answers from the weavers, *A Brief State of the Question* (1719), *The Weavers' True Case* (1719), by Claudius Rey, a Weaver (called " Monsieur Rey " in the *British Merchant*), and *The Just Complaints of the Poor Weavers* (1719) supposed to be by Daniel Defoe.† These bulky pamphlets argued that the complaint was not made by Spitalfields alone, but by the whole nation, and laid down the following four propositions :

(1) That the woollen and silk manufactures " being the staple of our trade . . . the fund of our exportation, the support of our navigation, the only means we have for the employing and supporting our poor, it is therefore the common interest of the Kingdom to discourage any other manufacture whether foreign or assumed so far as those manufactures are ruinous to and inconsistent to the prosperity of the said British Manufactures " ;

(2) That the wearing of printed and painted calicoes was ruinous to and inconsistent with the prosperity of English manufactures ;

(3) East India Trade can go on even though those are prohibited ; and that

(4) The clandestine importations can only be stopped by prohibiting the wear of calicoes. These four propositions put the case of the weavers in a nutshell.

The weavers' opponents were by no means silenced. *A Further Examination of the Weavers' Pretences* (1719) maintained that calicoes did not harm woollens and that the damp in trade at the time was caused rather by the avarice of the weavers in taking too many apprentices. The linen-printers in *The Essay on Trade* (1719) made out that England

* Lee, II, p. 184.
† Gold. Libr. ac. to Prof. Foxwell.

may, by encouraging their industry, "become the peer of other linen-manufacturing countries," the linen drapers also published a separate *Reply* in which they showed that owing to the riots calico stagnated in their shops, and were not demanded at all.

Calico-chasing was still going on in the city, especially towards the evenings. Numerous cases are reported in the newspapers during the months of July, August and September, 1719. Weavers mercilessly ill-treated all those they found wearing calicoes, and sometimes even threw *aqua fortis* on their clothes. Women were thereby much offended by the weavers, and some of them were made desperate. On July 29th, when Humphreys and others were standing in pillory at Spitalfields, three women came in a coach dressed in calicoes and drove round the pillory as if they meant to insult the weavers. Some of the weavers, perceiving this, gathered about the coach and " stripped them as clean of the calicoes as a butcher does a partridge of its feathers."* Similar cases again occurred on the same day, It is reported that weavers even got into people's houses to hunt for calicoes, and this " at the very doors of magistrates."† When they seized any calicoes they carried them in triumph on the tops of poles and sticks. In order to show that they were not seditious, they cried " King George for Ever " when they assembled. Some women boldly resisted the weavers and had very narrow escapes. One scandalous fellow, " noted for his songs and catches against the Government," went into the meetings of Protestant dissenters in Spitalfields and bred disturbance there. He was seized and was ordered by the Justices to Newgate Prison.‡

These disturbances did not last much longer than October. This was partly due to the action taken by Government, but it was also due to the fact that winter having set in, people began to use their woollen goods. It is significant that the riots broke out in midsummer, when people naturally preferred to wear light clothing. This

* *Weekly Journal or British Gazetteer*, August 1.
† *Weekly Journal or Saturday Post*. July 11.
‡ *Flying Post*, August 8.

fact also gives us the right clue as to the extent of the use of calicoes in England. In summer most people wore it, but in winter it was little used. There was therefore little chance of riots breaking out after October.

Nor were these riots confined to London. Norwich acted in concert with Spitalfields. In the middle of June there was a rumour that the Norwich* weavers were coming in a body to meet their London brethren, but it never came about. A calico-chase took place every now and then during the months of July and August. In September† a serious riot broke out. The rabble cut down calico gowns into pieces from women's backs, entered shops in search of calico and assaulted the constables who came to stop them. At last the authorities raised the Artillery Company, and the rising was quelled.

Women complained bitterly of ill-treatment and Defoe gave expression to their views in his paper. " We are oppressed and insulted here in open streets and frighted, stript, our clothes torn off our backs every day by the rabbles. . . . Never tell us of national liberties ; if our sex has not a share in these liberties, how can it be called national ? "‡ According to Mist, many women resolved " to wear nothing that is weav'd in Spittlefields."

The Whig and Tory newspapers continued to attack each other on the question. Later on, the parties felt the need of separate journals for themselves. First came out the *Manufacturer* and then the *Weaver* to argue on the side of the weavers. These weekly papers were answered by a rival organ, the *British Merchant*, which stood for a cause the very reverse of the programme of its earlier namesake. The contents of these papers were couched in the most scurrilous language. Especially the latter journal contained little except personal attacks, a specimen of which being that its opponent " could hardly pay the rent of a garret in

---

* *Weekly Journal of Saturday Post*, June 20.

† Blomfield, *History of Norfolk*, II, p. 209, puts it in 1721 ; but evidently this ought to be 1720 ; in 1721 (Sept.) there could hardly have been any provocation for such riots.

‡ *Saturday Post*, August 15.

Grub Street." Such venomous language was of course not uncommon in the days of Pope and Swift.

Many ballads were composed in order to rouse the country against the use of calicoes.

> " Now our trade is so bad,
> That the weavers run mad
> Thro' the want of both work and provisions,
> That some hungry poor rogues
> Feed on grains like hogs,
> They are reduced to such wretched conditions,
> Then well may they teare
> What our ladies weare
> And foes to their country upbraid them,
> Till none shall be thought
> A more scandalous slut
> Than a tawdry Callico-Madam."

Some clever writer composed an *Elegy on the Death of Trade*, in which he represented Trade as a distressed dame going and begging for help from all the quarters in the city, including the East India House, and receiving unfair treatments everywhere.

> " An honest old dame,
> Mother *Trade* was her name,
> That had long laid in despair state
> Perceiving at last
> That all hopes they were past,
> Most contentedly yielded to fate."

III

The Weavers' Grievances

One obvious cause of the disturbances described in the last section was unemployment and all the resulting ills thereof. We must first survey the extent of the misery and then enquire into its causes.

The chief place affected was Spitalfields, the centre of the silk industry at the time. It began to flourish rapidly after the Act of 1700. The industry revived and employed numerous hands, and silk weaving spread to neighbouring places like Hoxton, Stepney, Southwark and Canterbury.

It was estimated that two million pounds worth of silks were made there annually. By 1719, however, the industry again "fell into decay and the poor were reduced to the same necessities as before the Prohibition."* The weavers made most exaggerated statements about their sufferings. For example, it was stated that a great "many poor manufacturers being wholly destitute of work and consequently of subsistence, have been found dead in the streets and fields, where they have perished of mere want and cold."† This statement is doubtless exaggerated, but it is based upon some truth, as in the case of most pamphlets of the time. Even Defoe, who has an unquestionable right to our respect, wrote in 1719 : "Whole families are reduced almost to the extremity of starving for want of work and there is such a decay of their trade that if the calicoes are allowed to be worn ; . . . a 100,000 families must find some other employment or be kept by the country to the excessive burden of the nation, or perish."‡

The testimony of prominent employers of labour is important in the matter. Mr. Edes had been employing 180 to 230 looms in making callimancoes and cambletta partly for exportation. But by 1719 he had to reduce his trade "to the compass of less than 100 looms and even those not fully employed."§ Even according to Mr. Edes's "modest calculation" of his own factory, fifteen hundred men, women and children were out of employment. His memorial was made at the request of the Trade Commissioners and his statements deserve special credit.

Mercers and other traders complained that their goods would not sell. Blackwell Hall "lay piled up to the roofs with goods and the whole-men's factories and warehouses were thronged with them."

Nor was London the only place affected. All centres of worsted and silk industries had really a bad time. In 1720 petitions came from all over England complaining of the

* Public Record Office, C.O. 389, vol. XXIX, p. 235.
† Brit. Mus. 816 m. 14, No. 84.
‡ *Weekly Journal of Saturday Post*, August 8.
§ See his memorial, C.O. 398, Vol. XXVIII, p. 224.

havoc wrought by calicoes ; but many of them were drawn
up by interested parties. However it is certain that Norwich
and Canterbury suffered almost as much as Spitalfields. In
Canterbury, according to a petition to the Trade Commissioners, looms were reduced from 1,000 to 100. Norwich,
too, according to the chronicles of the city, suffered very
much.*

When the weavers began to complain of unemployment
one William Smith advertised in the *London Gazette* (June 13)
that weavers would be employed in his sail-cloth factories
at Reading and Hoxton, in making sails for His Majesty's
Navy. Defoe considered it only as an attempt at holding
oneself up as a patriot whilst bringing down the price of
journeymen ; nor could he understand how woollen weavers
could do the work of linen-making without special training
for it. †

Even in those times the various trades and industries
were inter-related and when one suffered, the others were
sure to be disturbed. The Italian and Turkey trades were
very much cut down. Unemployed workmen looked to
parishes for support. According to a pamphlet, women and
children were left to parishes and their husbands and fathers,
not being able to bear the cries which they could not relieve,
" are fled to France and other Countries to seek their
bread."‡

The latter statement deserves special attention. Many
writers of the time complain of the migration of " the more
ingenious of the artisans " to foreign countries. The Trade
Commissioners were specially interested in the question and
owing to their energetic enquiries, we have now got many
documents on the subject. The country to which any
considerable number of men went was France, and it came
about under peculiar circumstances. That arch-schemer
John Law, put it into the heads of the French that they could
plant a woollen industry and thereby compete successfully
with England. He himself seems to have started a factory

---

* Blomfield, Vol. II, p. 307.
† *Just Complaints of the Poor Weavers*, p. 15.
‡ 816 m. 14, *op. cit.*

at his residence at Tankerville. An English clothier named John Paget was employed by him to " decoy " English artificers and " so learn the French our manner of making cloth and druggets." According to a memorial submitted before the Commissioners* on September 20, 1720, Paget persuaded twenty English workmen to go to France on the pretence that they were being taken to Scotland. At the same time Mrs. Paget was active in London persuading distressed labourers to go to France.

In November, 1719, the Commissioners received many depositions on the subject. William Ellicombe, woolcomber at Shoreditch, informed them how a man " in the appearance of a gentleman, who called himself John Brown, read a letter at a tavern in Newgate to some people, intimating that several English artificers who were lately arrived in France were mighty well pleased with their living there ! " The deponent himself was invited to go and was given a guinea. Similar statements were received also from Mr. Edes a ' manufacturer,' Thomas Piggot of Whitehall, Michael Cleare of Stepney. Cleare stated that several persons had gone to France, with their implements. According to Edes, a few weavers had gone also to Switzerland, and the excellent Callimancoes they made there had already come to England. All these were most alarming news in those days, when national rivalries were very keen—when the prosperity of foreign countries was looked upon as detrimental to the interests of the home country.

All these evils were doubtless due to unemployment, but how did this come about ? The weavers and those who supported their cause maintained that the use of calicoes was the root cause of all the misery. And thus the whole blame was laid at the door of the two classes of people interested in calicoes—the East India Company that brought the calicoes, and the printers who worked them up. The popular conception was that calicoes directly displaced woollens and silks. " So much as is consumed of Indian calicoes, whether white or printed," wrote one pamphleteer, "just so much of our manufactures are less consumed, and so much as is less

* Public Record Office, C.O., 389, vol. 2.

consumed of our manufactures just so much of our people's labour is taken away."* Defoe put it in even more graphic language : " the calicoes and woollen manufactures being like two balances, when one scale went down the other went up, and when one went up the other went down."†

This was vehemently denied by the weavers' opponents. They maintained that owing to the heavy duties charged, printed calicoes had become too dear to compete with woollen goods. Only a third of the calicoes printed were used for wearing, and the rest were either exported or used for furniture. The calicoes used never displaced woollens ; and as for silk it was admitted that it suffered a little, but silk was as much foreign as calico. *The British Merchant* challenged its opponents to show what woollens were displaced by calicoes, and the *Manufacturer* took up the challenge, but nothing was actually proved.

The calico-printers and others attributed the unemployment to the avarice of master-weavers and the idleness of workmen. It was pointed out that they had employed too many apprentices, "swarms of raw boys strolling about under the pretence of wanting work." Many of the new employees were idle men. " When they have a flush of work in the spring then many of them will not work above three days in the week, running away to alehouses, drinking and gaming away their money, . . . so that it is no wonder that their families may want when the time of ebb comes."

These causes could not sufficiently explain the acute unemployment of the time. As a general cause, the latter may be pointed out, but it cannot explain the trouble under consideration. As for the employment of too many apprentices, the Commissioners' enquiry brought out that only 3,213 apprentices were taken during the period 1709-1717, about 300 on an average for each year. There is, however, a grain of truth in the allegation, for we find that after 1716, greater numbers were apprenticed. Yet this, too, could not sufficiently explain the acute unemployment that then prevailed.

* *Weavers' True Case*, p. 6.
† *Just Complaints*, p. 15.

What then were the real causes ? No doubt the increased use of calicoes did interfere to some extent with the demand for woollens and silks ; but this cannot be assigned as the sole cause of the misery. Defoe himself admitted that there were " other causes of the present damp upon their trade,"* but he would not specify them. However, we learn some from other sources. First, there was going on at the time a war with Spain, which must have dislocated foreign trade to some extent. Spain and Spanish colonies were important customers of England in those days, and besides all trade is inter-dependent. Add to this also the strained relations with Russia, and other Continental complications aggravated by the Hanoverian interests of George I. That was a time when Sunderland and Stanhope were grappling with those knotty problems of European diplomacy. We need not enter into details here.

Secondly we must also remember that it was a time of trade crisis, and such cyclic fluctuations used to occur in the eighteenth century as well. Besides the unrest arose during that part of the year when trade was bound to be slack.

The Directors of the Company pointed out that the unemployment of the time was due also to " manufactures shifting to other places."† The results of such migrations are well-known.

Nevertheless, the whole blame was laid on calicoes, and even Government lent support to this prejudiced view.

IV

The Case before Government.

When the weavers' riots broke out, Parliament was not in session ; and therefore the weavers could not apply immediately for redress. However, the London weavers soon put in a petition before the Lords Justices stating their case in forcible language. The Justices referred the petition to the Lords Commissioners of Trade and Plantations, as

* *Saturday Post*, June 27. Lee, II, p. 136.
† Board of Trade, Petitions, C.O. Q. 143.

they were the proper body to move in the matter. And really this was a happy step.

The Commissioners of the time were an energetic body. Without their active co-operation Parliament would not have been able to carry on a protectionist policy successfully. They were the economic guardians of the Kingdom and their eye was everywhere. Nothing of any consequence to English economic interests escaped their attention. The rumour comes that Germany has started a woollen industry, and at once they are roused to activity to get all details of the new venture and to safeguard England's interest in the matter. Then comes another, about the "decoying" away of English artificers, and again they are all energy. This wonderful body was the real embodiment of the policy of Parliamentary Colbertism throughout the eighteenth century. They had effective agencies for all kinds of enquiries in foreign countries and exerted themselves vigorously for securing the interests of England abroad. The principal commissioners at the time were the Duke of Westmoreland, Lord Chetwynd, Charles Cooke, P. Dominique, Thomas Pelham and Mr. Baden; and they had an energetic secretary in Thomas Popple. Even though their champion Pollexfen had been removed by death, the weavers found in them a body anxious to redress their grievances.

As soon as the petition of the weavers was received, the Commissioners set in motion the whole machinery at their command. They at once wrote to prominent people, connected with the various trades, to Sir Gerard Cornniers of the Turkey Company, and to Mr. Peter Lekeux of Spital-fields, to Sherwell, Badcock and other mercers in London, and to prominent manufacturers like Mr. Edes and Mr. Tidmarsh, and asked them to communicate their views on the subject of the weavers' petition. They also approached the Customs Office and other Government agencies for various facts and figures connected with the subject. Nor did they neglect the opposite side. The East India Company was asked to submit an explanation, and similarly the prominent calico-printers and linen-drapers too were allowed to have their say.

The replies received by them and the memorials submitted supply us with the most valuable details of the state of trade and industries at the time.

On December 12 they submitted their report to the King, in which they took a comprehensive survey of the whole question. Though they were not able to probe very deep into the causes of the complaint, they made out that calicoes actually harmed English manufactures and expressed the conviction that the wearing of such goods must be restrained in the interests of the staple industries of the realm. They accepted it as a truism that whatever came in the way of the woollen industry was to be removed, and they had not enough insight to see that calico-painting too was an industry of the Kingdom. They neglected its claims completely and perhaps one reason for this was the fact that most of the printers were Roman Catholics, as they stated in their report. The Commissioners finally suggested that a law might be made to prohibit the wearing of printed calicoes, " as they had done in France to the great advantage of that Kingdom."

Meantime the weavers' petitions had reached Parliament. The first of them* was received on November 24 from the Incorporated Company of Clothiers of Worcester, setting forth that " the clothing trade joining with the rest of the woollen manufactures of the Kingdom had for many years last past been the greatest support of the landed interest, the employing of the poor and the strength of the nation ; that the said trade is on a very declining condition, and many thousands of poor families ready to perish for want of labour, which is occasioned by exportation of wool to foreign markets and by wearing of calicoes and stained linens in Great Britain ; which if not timely prevented may be of fatal consequence, by forcing many thousands of workmen to foreign parts and ruin many thousands of good families who have hitherto employed the poor ; and the poor in general must perish."

From December 1, the House was actually flooded with petitions. They came from all parts of Great Britain and represented all classes comprised in the woollen, worsted and

---

* *Commons Journals*, XIX, p. 168.

silk industries. There were about ninety petitions in all. Some places like London, Norwich, Canterbury, Worcester and Gloucester, sent many petitions representing various classes employed in the industry. The town corporations of most places participated in the petitions and in some cases the weavers and spinners represented their grievances separately. Besides weavers and spinners, other classes also were represented in the petitions: woolcombers, silk-throwers, serge-makers, flannel-makers, dyers, stiffeners, clothiers, mercers, websters, drugget-makers, and retail tradesmen. From some places the petitions were chiefly from gentlemen who were affected by the rise of poor rates. From Gloucester,* the Justices of the Peace sent in a separate petition informing the House that they would soon become bankrupt by poor relief.

The House was really very much concerned. First it had the interests of the Kingdom at heart ; and in those days, Parliament jealously safeguarded the security of industries. In the present case, however, there was even a more urgent reason for the House to move ; for the interests of the gentry were at stake in so far as the price of wool fell and the poor rates rose exceedingly.

Some of the petitions, however, were the work of agitators. The Company was on the alert to expose such matters. It pointed out that the broadcloth industry of Worcester was least affected by the consumption of calicoes. Dunwich had no weavers at all, and yet a petition was received from that place. It is likely that some weavers from London went about the country encouraging people to petition. At any rate, the language of the petitions is suspiciously uniform.

Anyhow the House was set in motion. All the petitions were referred to a Committee. In the middle of December they petitioned the King to order the Commissioners of Trade to place their report and papers before the House. The Customs officials also were asked to place their accounts on the table.

On January 14 the House resolved itself into a committee to consider the case, with Mr. Cartaret as chairman. They

* *Op. cit.*, p. 176.

heard the petitioners and also received representations from calico-printers, linen-drapers, merchants, and the East India Company. The most prominent figure among the petitioners was " the bold Norwich Quaker," John Gurney,* who,

> " To each House with its speaker
> When the spirit moved told the tale,
> And made it out fully
> That callicoes truly
> Endangered the good common weal."†

The calico-printers' contention was that they developed the art of printing and made it a new manufacture profitable to the Kingdom and employing many thousands of people, and that they had raised costly establishments, all of which would go to rot if calicoes were prohibited. The Scottish linen manufacturers made out even a stronger case. In a petition that came from " the Linen Manufacturers of that part of Great Britain called Scotland," they maintained that their manufacture was as ancient as the woollen, " much ancienter, than many of those about which some tumult and noise have been lately made,"‡ (meaning, of course, the silk industry of Spitalfields). Linen was to Scotland what wool was to England. If anything happened to it, they said, it would go against the terms of the Act of Union of 1707. Besides they boldly threatened to turn to woollen manufacture if linen failed. And this threat was calculated to frighten English weavers more than anything else. No wonder that linen was excepted from the provisions of the Bill of 1720. In marked contrast to the proud language of linen-makers came the humble appeal of the drapers whose " whole trade seemed stagnated owing to the late violent insults " on calico-wearers.

The East India Directors also put their case before Parliament. Already they had begun to intrigue with members of Parliament in order to form an interest for

---

* The Gurneys were an ancient Norfolk family (Blomfield, Vol. X, pp. 224-27). Norwich was a centre of Quakers at the time (Vict. Cty, Hist. Norfolk, Vol. II, p. 301-2.

† *Elegy on the Death of Trade,* 1720.

‡ Folio 666. Also Boyer *Political State,* XX, 100.

themselves in the House.* They claimed that they had a right to the India trade which they had bought dear by advancing above three million pounds at a time of great extremity, and that their trade was profitable to the country. Their chief settlements were in the " Calico countreys " and " if calico was prohibited in England they (i.e., the Company) would become contemptible in India." Besides, they pointed out that Indians would retaliate. " On hearing of the Prohibition of 1700 " they wrote " the (Indian) Governor of the Country near the Fort† threatened such a prohibition and the Company had to buy greater quantities to persuade that it was a false report."

On February 12, the Committee resolved that the " use of all printed, stained and dyed calicoes and linens in apparel household furniture and otherwise, except such as are the produce of Great Britain and Ireland, be prohibited after a certain time to be appointed." A Bill was ordered to be drawn up by Cartaret, Chancellor of the Exchequer, Sir Robert Walpole and others. On March 1, a Bill was introduced " for encouraging and preserving the woollen and silk manufactures of this Kingdom and for the more effectual employing of the poor by prohibiting the use and wear of all printed, painted, stained or dyed calicoes and linen except such as are the growth and manufacture of Great Britain and Ireland."

The Bill soon passed the lower House and was sent to the upper. The Lords too heard many parties interested in the affair. But on some pretext the Lords wanted to put off the question for six weeks. This alarmed the weavers as in 1697, and they were roused to action. They came in a riotous manner to Westminster, with their wives and children, 3,000 in all, and crowded the passages of the House of Lords and demanded justice of the Lords as they passed by. Their Lordships were frightened and lifeguards were called for, upon which the weavers returned to Spitalfields without making further disturbance. With a view to pacifying the weavers, the Lords addressed the Crown to ask the Trade Commissioners to prepare a scheme for prohibiting

* *Weekly Medley*, July 25.
† Fort St. George (Madras).

the wearing of calicoes, but also " to consider of and state the many difficulties the East India Company do at present lye under, in the carrying on of their trade." The King consented to do both, and immediately the address and the answer were published and spread broadcast. Parliament was soon adjourned.

Apparently the House of Lords was much interested in the safety of the Company, and certainly many of the Lords were concerned in the Joint-Stock itself. Even apart from that, the interests of the nation were bound up to a certain extent with the interests of the East India Trade. The Trade Commissioners, on receiving the command of the King, asked the Company to lay before them proposals for safeguarding its trade after the prohibition of calicoes in England. The Company asked for various privileges, as for example : (1) a law to discourage those trading under foreign commissions from Ostend and other places ; (2) the prompt payment of five per cent. out of the fifteen per cent. additional duty laid on its imports ; (3) grant of a longer period for drawbacks ; (4) the prohibition of the importation of East India goods to British Colonies except from Great Britain ; and (5) many privileges connected with the search of goods in the seas, with a view to crush contraband trade. The Commissioners recommended most of these to the King ; and some were eventually granted to the Company.

The Commissioners also enquired of the weavers how their business was prospering. Optimistic answers were received from most centres. They were "much fuller employed " than before. This was partly due to the passing of the crisis, and partly also to the greater demand for woollens in winter.

The ladies in London were very much annoyed at the possibility of not being allowed the use of calicoes and other beautiful printed goods. They thought that they would be worried to death when such a law came into force. The weavers addressed a " Humble Address " to the ladies to explain that they (the weavers) would not ill-treat the ladies and that they would only inform the Magistrate when they came to know that anyone used calico.

Newspapers were still violently attacking each other. *The British Merchant* and the *Manufacturer* still retailed cheap scandal and did not spare each other. Early in March the *British Merchant* lost hopes and was no more published, but the *Manufacturer* continued in triumph for some time more, and praised the Parliament profusely. Various pamphlets also appeared about the same time, *The Female Manufacturer's Complaint* (1720), and the *Spinster in Defence of the Woollen Manufactures* (1727) (ascribed to Steele) represented the grievances of the women of Spitalfields, who had of late become even more violent than the men.* Those pamphlets were satires upon calico-wearing ladies. They were partly answered by the *Linnen Spinster in Defence of Linnen Manufactures*. More serious pamphlets also appeared at the time, like David Clayton's *A Short System of Trade*, a citizens' *The Interest of the Nation Considered*, and the anonymous but forcible treatise, *The Trade to India Calmly and Critically Considered*, besides numerous broadsides on both sides. All the three pamphlets above named were subtle statements of the mercantilist position, written in the broader interests of national power rather than the narrow self-interest of the weavers, and as such they were valuable contributions to the controversy.

V

Prohibition and After

When Parliament assembled again, the first question that awaited attention was the " Calico Bill." Almost the whole nation was for passing the Bill, and Parliament even in those days sometimes gave way to popular clamour. When the Bill passed, the whole nation rejoiced. The *Manufacturer* soared to its highest pitch of eloquence when it wrote ; " From this day we may date the resurrection from the dead, as well of our foreign declining commerce as of our home manufactures," and it gloried in " the felicity of being born Britons."

* Lee, *Defoe*, III, 90-92.

The Act* that passed was a simpler document than that of 1700. Its preamble recounted only the decay of woollen manufactures and the excessive increase of the poor and did not commit itself to the bullionist position. It forbade the use or wear in Great Britain after December 25, 1722, of "printed, painted, stained and dyed callicoes" in any garment or apparel whatever and the use of the same on any bed, chair, cushion, under-cushion, or other household stuff whatever. The operation of the Act extended to "all stuffs made of cotton or mixed therewith, which shall be printed and painted with any colour or colours, or chequered or striped, or stitched or flowered in foreign parts with any colour or colours or with coloured flowers made there," but excepted muslins, neckcloths, fustians and calicoes dyed all blue (clauses I, X, and XI).

The penalties imposed were manifold. The offender would forfeit to the informer the sum of £5 in lawful money of Great Britain for every offence complained of within six days and convicted before a Justice of the Peace, and this sum would be levied by distress. Mercers, drapers, upholders or any other persons or corporation who sold or exposed for sale any of the prohibited goods (unless for exportation thereof) would lose his or their office, besides forfeiting the above sum. Every such offender would also forfeit £20, which would be divided equally between the informers or the prosecutor, and the poor of the Parish where the offence was committed. Persons so convicted might be taken away from any "pretended privileged place."

These penalties, however, did not apply to the calicoes already made up in bed or other household furniture before December 25, 1722. The result of this provision was that ladies soon "pulled down their calico gowns to pieces to make them into quilts and furniture covers."† Women could still use muslins and calicoes dyed all blue, and this must have been a great consolation for them.

About the same time France too made her prohibition more stringent. In spite of the earlier edicts printed

* 7 George I. Capt. V. Statutes at Large, Vol. V, p. 229.
† *Social England*, V, p. 185.

calicoes had become very popular in the early eighteenth century. "Fruit défendu" (writes M. Clouzot) "les toiles deviennent la passion de toutes les filles d'Eve francaises."* About half the people of France are said to have worn them. In 1709, the "Deputes du Commerce" violently complained of it and Louis XV issued an Edict in 1726 making the penalties much more severe than before. Smuggling was to be met with capital punishment on the third offence. Calico was similarly prohibited in all countries of Europe except Holland.

Nevertheless the forbidden fruit was still the passion of fashionable people. The wives of ministers were the first to break the law. Madame de Pompadour furnished a chateau at Belleville with the prohibited goods. Smuggling was practised openly, and depots for "indiennes" were established at Fontaineableau, Versailles and other aristocratic centres. The Government gradually realised the folly and the futility of its policy and the prohibition edicts were annulled in 1757.

Nor was the law much more successful in England. At first women were afraid to wear the prohibited goods, but soon they got over it. As early as 1723, Defoe† found women wearing prohibited goods, and he also records how such women were treated. In 1728 the same writer still complains of the passion of women for calicoes.‡ "All the Kings and Parliaments that have been or shall be," he wrote, "cannot govern our fancies . . . Two things among us are too ungovernable, viz., our passions and our fashions . . . Should I ask the ladies whether they would dress by law . . . they would ask me whether they were statute fools and to be made pageants and pictures of? . . ." Another patriotic writer§ about the same time condemned the madness of his country-women in turning their backs upon their own manufactures and running after the "thin painted old sheets" from India.

* Baker, *Calico Printing and Painting*, p. 67.
† Lee, III, p. 90-92.
‡ *A Plan of English Commerce* (1728), p. 252
§ *A Short Dedication of the Original, Progress and Immense Increase of English Woollen Manufactures* (1727).

How did the people get these goods after 1721? In the first place, muslins were not prohibited by the Act; and a great deal of the best cotton goods came under the name of muslins. Chintz was prohibited, and smuggling was the only means of running it into the country. And the English traders in India found means to send in a good deal of such goods every year in spite of all the vigilance of Customs House officials. The best example of such smuggling is supplied by the bed of David Garrick, now at the South Kensington Museum. The great actor sent some play scenes to friends at Calcutta, and "a rather better in return" they sent madeira wine to him and a nice chintz bed to Mrs. Garrick. The latter was somehow smuggled in and was in use for some time in their pretty house at Hampton, but later, owing to some treachery "it was seized, the very bed, by the coarse hands of filthy dungeon villains, and thrown amongst ye smuggled lumber."* Mr. Garrick wrote an interesting letter to Guy Cooper of the Custom House, and the correspondence that ensued can be examined at the above-mentioned museum. Mr. Cooper also wrote an equally interesting letter. "Upon such occasions," he wrote, "I hate Acts of Parliament more than ever, and I wish the Custom House and all their regulations, rules and forms . . . all at the devil." He promised to exert all his influence "as if the present had been from the Nabob of Oudh to Our Most Gracious Queen." Garrick got it back and it graced their house at Hampton for long. Similar cases of smuggling occurred now and then.

The East India Company still went on dealing in manufactured cotton goods from India. The importation of white calico had reached very high figures from 1718 to 1720 —exactly at the time of the uproar against these goods. From 676,082 pieces in 1717, it soared to 1,220,324 pieces in 1718, and 2,088,451 pieces in 1719; but in 1722, it suddenly fell to 718,678 pieces, obviously owing to the Prohibition Act. In 1721, the directors wrote to Calcutta to cut down earlier orders owing to the prohibition, which is but faintly referred to there. Yet the Company went on

* Letter dated June 2, 1775.

increasing investments as before and until the middle of the century, the imports show little reduction. Many of their imports were re-exported either to the Continent or to the Colonies, where the Company still had an unrestrained market. After 1745, the Indian goods show a lowering in quality and gradually the demand for them fell off. The critical years in this process of decay were 1750-52. After 1752, indents ceased for a time, and the trade in Indian chintz practically stopped. Muslins were still popular and continued so until equally good stuff came to be made in Manchester. Yet, until the sixties of the last century, Indian goods continued to be imported unto England, though in small quantities.

The calico-printing industry was certainly very much harmed by the prohibition Act; yet the printers still went on printing fustians and linens. Even cotton they could print for exportation, and they actually did so. Nor did they lack a market for it in England.* Thus a great impetus was given to linen and fustian printing about this time. In 1728, Defoe noted that the Act of 1720 had not resulted in the revival of the woollen industry as was expected, but "the humour of the people running another way the callico-printers fell to work to imitate those callicoes by making the same stamps and impressions, and with the same beauty of colours."†

By the middle of the century English printers became highly skilled in their art. In 1744, the Directors wrote to India: "Printing here hath come to so great perfection that unless you can keep to these instructions you must lessen the quantity." About the same time‡ a calico printer of Bayle, Jean Rymer, praised the English printers for having surpassed their Dutch teachers in excellence. "It was reserved for the English," he wrote, "to attempt the imitation of the best Indian work in prints and to arrive at a degree of perfection which no one would have thought possible." In 1754 the English chintz which a dealer presented to the

* Dr. Knowles, *Industrial and Commercial Revolutions* (1922), p. 45.
† *A Plan of English Commerce*, p. 296.
‡ Baker, op. cit., p. 38.

Princess of Wales is said to have greatly excelled Indian chintz in workmanship.*

It took still a long time for printing to be introduced into Lancashire, its present home. Messrs. Clayton began printing on a small scale at Preston in 1764, but it was Robert Peel, the grandfather of the Prime Minister, that established the first great factory for calico-printing. Peel developed the industry, and Baines truly says that " Peel was to calico-printing what Arkwright was to spinning."

The weavers did not like the new turn that the industry took after 1721. As early as 1723, the Spitalfields weavers ill-treated those who wore printed linen, even though those were not prohibited by law. Defoe writes most humorously of these street outrages in which often he was himself a party. The women of Spitalfields took an active part in the propaganda, and when told that linen was also an "English manufacture," and was not prohibited, they said, " our manufacture ! No, no, they are not our Spitalfields manufacture." So narrow was the outlook of those weavers. "Spitalfields alone must be provided," wrote Defoe sarcastically, " and all the rest starved."

The Norwich weavers became even more aggressive about 1730. They persecuted fustian printers and weavers, and inserted notices in newspapers that wearing printed fustians was illegal. They had even the audacity to institute prosecutions on the Act of 1720. The fustian manufacturers were annoyed and petitioned Parliament and claimed protection for their ancient fustian manufacture. Lancashire, for the first time, took the lead in this affair. The result was the " Manchester Act " of 1735, which laid down that printed goods of linen yarn and cotton wool manufactured in Great Britain were excluded from the operation of the Act of 1720.

The ban put upon cotton was bound to be ineffective. As Dr. Lilian Knowles points out the prohibition of foreign cotton cloth gave a strong impulse to the invention of spinning machinery in England.† People of all sorts and

---

* Baines, op. cit., p. 261.
† Knowles, *Industrial and Commercial Revolutions*, p. 43.

conditions had got accustomed to the use of light and elegant cotton clothing, and even Parliament had not the power effectively to withhold such goods from them. And necessity, as ever, became the mother of invention. Barely twelve years after the prohibition, John Kay invented the fly-shuttle for weaving, and within thirty years of that Hargreaves, Arkwright and Crompton made their epoch-making inventions by which spinning was incredibly facilitated and cheapened. And what was even more important, yarn strong enough to serve for warp was made for the first time in England, and thereby it was made possible for genuine cotton cloth to be made in vast quantities in that country.* This decided that Lancashire was henceforth to be the world's cotton factory. Under these circumstances it was impossible to continue the ban on cotton goods. A statute of 1774 legalised "the new manufacture made entirely of cotton spun in the kingdom," but the duty remained until 1830.

Thus in spite of the rigours of mercantilism and the nation's steadfast devotion to wool, cotton became the staple industry of England and ousted wool from its premier place. By the middle of the nineteenth century, cotton became what wool once was—the palladium of national prosperity. And Sydney Smith was bold enough to write as early as 1845 : " The great object for which the Anglo-Saxon race appears to have been created is the making of calico."†

---

* The cotton goods made in England were not called by any new names but adopted the Indian names (e.g., calico, chintz, muslin) long familiar in the country.

† Works, III, p. 476.

APPENDIX A.

Specimens of the Directors' Order for Goods from India

I. Bengal.

List of Goods to be provided in y Bay sent with Despatch to Bengal Dec. 21, 1683, by Ship " Resolution."

At Ballazoar (Ballasore).

Ginghams colored of y finest sort and not stiff all of cloth colors	20,000	Pieces
Silk and Romalls better than this year not stiffened	20,000	,,
Nillaes of good colors	36,000	,,
Sannaes as many as possible you can of y sort No. 1 by the Defence	40,000	,,
Herba Taffeties of cloth colⁿ lively collors	6,000	,,
Herba Longis	20,000	,,
Saryaes of severall collⁿ 10 yard long and one yard wide to be made thicker than usual	4,000	,,
Send no Tassera or Herba Thread or Yarn.		
Cotton yarn not hard spun or coss	500	bales
Sticklack	100	tons
Cowries	100	tons
Board Blue Ginghams ordinary sort	100	tons
Herba stuffs 10 yards long and a yard wide of diverse cloth colours	2,000	Pieces
Any sort of new shifts of Herba or Cotton or silk and cotton of each for a trial	12	bales

At Pattana (Patna).

Saltpetre what more you can get	1,500	tons
Turmerick	200	tons

At Hughly.

Silk Romalls	50,000	Pieces
Sattins—vizᵗ. Pink coloⁿ ⎫ French Yellow ⎪ and other Skie ⎬ good colorˢ Crimson ⎭	16,000	Pieces

a fourth part to be rich and well covored

166

APPENDIX A

Mohobut Bannies to be made without y rice starch which rots them	1,500	Pieces
Allabannies	4,000	,,
Phota Longis	5,000	,,
Charconais fine	5,000	,,
(do.) ordinary	4,000	,,
Amorees	1,600	,,
Elatches of each sort	3,000	,,
Peniascoes of all cotton ¾ and silks ¼		
Charcolaes double pieces each 10 yards long and yard wide	8,000	,,
Sonsaes of severall colors 10 yards long and one yard wide	4,000	,,
Striped Mallmulls fine (Dorca) 21 yards long all wide best make at Hughli, Santapore and Maulda, some to be striped a little broader and some narrower than the pattern sent	8,000	,,
Atlasses to y' samples sent	8,000	,,
Ditto, Flowered white	1,000	,,
Silk Neckcloths	4,000	,,
Gold and silver stripes, 50 pieces of every sort		
Any sort of new stuffs of silk or silk and cotton either plain or striped is favered	20	bales
Diapers finest and strongest ¾ yd. wide	2,000	Pieces
Table cloths 2½ yards wide	200	,,
Dimities finest	2,000	
Opium of the best	24	Duppers
Silk Quilts	2	tons
Sealing wax	2	tons
Silk Quilts	2,000	Pieces
Chandannies	10,000	,,
Orungshies	2,000	,,
Chawtaras	10,000	,,
Umber Charconais	8,000	,,
Umbers	4,000	,,

At Dacca

Cassaes fine	13,000	Pieces
Malmulls of all sorts fine and coarse	15,000	,,
Tanjeebs fine	6,000	,,
Seerbands fine ¾ yd. wide make them full yard wide if it can be	10,000	,,
Seersuccers	5,000	,,
Humhums fine	6,000	,,
Fine Adathics of each sort.	1,500	,,
Silk Romalls	10,000	,,

Malmulls with fine flowers wrought into white, the flowers to be about 3 or 4 inches asunder clean and neatly made 21 yds. long and ell wide   4,000 Pieces
Ditto striped   1,000 ,,
Any sort of new goods for tryall   12 bales
White silk what quantity can get.

AT MAULDA.

Cassaes fine	13,000	Pieces
Malmulls of all sorts fine and coarse, some finer than usual	15,000	,,
Tanjeebs fine	10,000	,,
Zeerbands fine ¾ yd. wide	5,000	,,
Seersuccers	4,000	,,
Rohings	3,000	,,
Humhums, fine	4,000	,,
Fine Adathies of each sort	15,000	,,
Silks and cotton striped stuff called Mandilla 22 yards long & ell wide, &c.	10,000	,,
Puttaes or Birds Eye (from Zeerpoor	2,000	,,
ditto. striped	3,000	,,
Striped Malmuls, fine Doreas (from Santaporee)	4,000	,,
Silk and cotton elasetics	12,000	,,
Any sort of new stuffs	20	bales

AT CASSIMBUZAR.

Taffaties	90,000	Pieces
Changeable collors	4,000	,,
Taffaties black strong and sound	15,000	,,
Ditto Green	1,500	,,
Ditto Skie	1,500	,,
Taffaties raw	10,000	,,
Taffaties either white or light ash to be dyed hard into blacks	6,000	,,
Striped Cheyn Taffaties	16,000	,,
Striped Taffaties or Rastaes	12,000	,,
Tarendines black	100	,,
Silk longees	20,000	,,
Chandebanns, good colors	6,000	,,
Shahazadees (10 yds. long 1 yd. wide)	2,000	,,
Sashes or girdles	4,000	,,
Sarsnets white	10,000	,,
Ditto black to a pattern formerly sent	5,000	,,
Any sort new stuffs	20	bales
Gold & silver stuffs 50 p of each		
Plushes and velvets of each sort	100	pieces

APPENDIX A

Raw silks, head & belly
   Ditto   ordinary
   White silk
   Yellow, &c.

What quantity you can get to y utmost

Floretta yarn of the finest sort   1,000 bales
Hundle cloth blew   1,000 pieces
   Ditto   brown
Thrown silk   200 bales
Shellack the best & finest Cassimbozer
     (Small miscellaneous items follow.)

(II) MADRAS.

List of Goods to be provided at the Coast, sent Dec. 12, 1683.
First jrny.

Long cloth ordinary	100,000	Pieces
Long cloth brown	40,000	,,
Longcloth fine	20,000	,,
Longcloth ordinary without stiffening	10,000	,,
Longcloth blew	20,000	,,
Sallampores ordinary	208,000	,,
Porcallaes fine	20,000	,,
Morees—various kinds	24,000	,,
Neckcloths—various sizes	24,000	,,
Neckcloth ordinary striped with red	300,000	,,
Ginghams ⅜ths broad	7,000	,,
Izarees made at y Fort for a trial	2,000	,,
Betellees	12,000	,,
Dimitees of the strongest & finest sorts can be made	5,000	,,
Diapers—different	5,000	,,
Cotton yarn accndg to sample	150	bales
Red wood red Saunders	300	bales

AT MECHLEPATAM, &C.

Long cloth	36,000	pieces
Salampores, 2 kinds	44,000	,,
Porcollers fine of Bettipolee	6,000	,,
Book Percollees	3,000	,,
Percollees of finest sorts made into chintz	4,000	,,
Colconda or Pettapollee coarse paintings	15,000	,,
Ginghams, white and brown	13,000	,,
Izarees	6,000	,,
Original Betellees	10,000	,,
Cumum Betellees to patern	20,000	,,
Gulcondah Betellees, very fine & thin	3,000	,,
Allejaes	24,000	,,

APPENDIX A

Saderuncheras	10,000	Pieces
Colloway Poos	10,000	,,
Sacerguntees	10,000	,,
Goacon Chazollar	16,000	,,
Dungarees	30,000	,,
Cotton Rumalls	100,000	,,
Sailcloth, if good	30,000	,,
Salampores	7,200	,,
Percollaes	1,800	,,
Cumums	16,000	,,
Pegu Sticklack	200	tons ·
Salpecados	4,000	prs.

III. SURAT

List of Goods to be provided at Surat, August, 1682.

Bufts, broad, white	120,000	Pieces
Do. browne	28,000	,,
Do. Blewe	24,000	,,
Do. Blew finest sort that is made	5,000	,,
Do. black with golden rowes	9,000	,,
Do. black such as Mr. Dicker sent	16,000	,,
Rafts, narrow, white	110,000	,,
Do. Browne	16,000	,,
Do. Brampore	2,600	,,
Chintz, broad to be new and neat	30,000	,,
Do. other patterns	20,000	,,
Do. narrow ½ ell wide	27,000	,,
do. serungee fine	36,000	,,
Do. coarse	20,000	,,
Do. caddy most striped with large figures	40,000	,,

(Other orders).

Indico Lahore—at the cheapest prices procurable	16,000 pounds.
Also Karmania Wood	800 bales.
Cardamons	400 bales.
Cushia lignum	600 bales &c.
Shellack, seedlack, &c.	
Nutmegs. Pepper, &c.	

APPENDIX B.

THE tradition (reported by McCulloch) that Henry Martyn was the author of this tract is supported by various evidences. Perhaps the most important of them is that in one of the copies preserved in the Goldsmiths' Library, we find the words "by Henry Martyn, Esq.," which, according to Prof. Foxwell, is in "apparently contemporary handwriting."* And all that we know of Martyn does not militate against this conclusion.

Henry Martyn, according to various authorities,† was the eldest son of Edward Martyn, of Upham in Wiltshire, and was the elder brother of Edward Martyn (Junior), Professor of Rhetoric as Gresham College from 1696 to 1720. Henry was educated at Eton, and perhaps Cambridge, and was called to the Bar. He was reputed to be an able lawyer as well as a talented writer, but owing to his failing health he seldom practised at the Bar. He wrote some good papers for the *Spectator*‡ about 1711-12, and its editor, Sir Richard Steele, esteemed his articles so much that he placed him at the head of his list of contributors, which included such names as Alexander Pope. Steele even declared that Martyn's name "can hardly be mentioned in a list wherein he would not deserve the precedence."§ Later he seems to have been one of the principal writers of the *British Merchant*, the Whig Journal that opposed the French trade negotiations of the Tory Ministry in 1712. When the Whigs came to power in 1715, his services were rewarded with the office of the Inspector-General of Exports and Imports. However, his literary successes and official preferments did not help his purse very much. When he died at Blackheath in 1721, he left vast debts, which were later paid off by his only son Bendal (Fellow of King's College, Cambridge) with the fortune left him by an aunt. ‖

At the outset the question arises how the author of such an avowed Free Trade tract as *The Considerations* could later become

---

* In a private letter.

† *Life of Gresham Professors* (1740), by John Ward (who himself succeeded Martyn as Gresham Professor in 1720), pp. 333-34.

‡ *Spectator*, Vol. VII, No. 555.

§ *Ibid*, Introduction to the Volume.

Harwood's *Alumni Etonensis*, p. 299.

the principal contributor to the *British Merchant*. This is an objection which apparently cannot be easily explained away. However we might remember that those were days when journalists changed sides with kaleidoscopic rapidity and even refuted under other names what they wrote under their own. But in the case of Martyn, we must seek for explanation in another quarter. It was not unusual in those days even among honest men to stand for liberal trade relations with one country while opposing the same in the case of another. There was, besides, an interval of twelve years between the *Considerations* (1701) and *The British Merchant* (1713); and this was evidently long enough to explain a change of views. Further, there are indications in the *British Merchant* that its authors viewed the Indian trade in an altogether different light from the French trade. Observe, for example, the following passage in that journal* :—" I very much question whether it ever could be objected against the trade of the East Indies, as has justly been against that of France, that it exhausted the treasure or lessened the value of the Native Commodities and manufactures of our realm."

Although the *Considerations* is apparently an impartial defence of a principle, it need not be supposed that the author had no self-interest in maintaining such a thesis. Almost every pamphlet on East Indian trade written in that period—especially from 1696 to 1700—was meant to promote the interests of party or faction. The English manufacturers and bullionists were pitted against Indian trade in general, and the interlopers were opposed to the old Company in particular. The *Considerations* was not definitely meant to serve any of these causes, yet it does not follow that the author had no interests in the matter. It is possible that he was in some way allied to the linen-drapers who, 1696-97, carried on an energetic controversy with Cary. There are striking resemblances between their pamphlets and the *Considerations*. For instance one of their pamphlets emphatically put the Free Trade position thus† :—" I affirm that it is the interest of England to send their products and manufactures to the best market, and from thence to bring such commodities as they cannot purchase cheaper anywhere else, and the remainder in money which they ought to lay out where they could buy cheapest and by the natural circulation the nation will be enriched," and concluded in the manner of the *Considerations* : " A Free Trade makes all manner of commodities cheap, the cheapness of commodities empowers our people to work cheaper, the cheapness of work encourages foreign trade, and foreign trade brings wealth and people, and that

---

* Vol. II. p. 144 ; also Vol. I, pp. 30-31.

† *Linen Drapers' Rejoinder* (813 M. 13, No. 143).

alone raises the price of land and houses.'' One cannot but connect this pamphlet with the author of the *Considerations*. We might remember in this connection that Henry Martyn's brother Richard was a linen-draper, and was, therefore, interested in the controversy.

The circumstances of the time offer an explanation why the author so carefully hid himself under the screen of anonymity. England in those days was vehemently for Protection, and anyone who expressed such an unpatriotic view as full-fledged Free Trade could not expect any promotion in public office. We read in the biography of Sir Dudley North, that even he, virulent Tory as he was, destroyed all the available copies of his work *Discourse on Trade*, in order to get rid of this printed evidence of the heterodoxy of his economic views.* Henry Martyn was apparently an aspirant for office and naturally he did not wish to spoil his chances by such a root-and-branch refutation of mercantilist policy.

Henry Martyn and his brother Richard were avowed Whigs and held office during the Whig régime. Apparently most of the linen-drapers, too, were Whigs. If Henry Martyn was really the author of the *Considerations*, as we have tried to show, it follows that Adam Smith was not the first Whig to preach free trade (*pace* Sir William Ashley).

---

* Roger North, *Lives of the Norths* (1826), p. 173.

APPENDIX C.

CALICO PRINTING IN SURREY

IT will be interesting to trace the further developments of the calico-printing industry which was first introduced into England about 1690 (see Chapter IV, Sec. II.)   In spite of the repressive legislation already noted, this new industry flourished in the counties of Surrey and Kent, until about the middle of the nineteenth century.   The banks of the river Wandle (tributary of the Thames) were studded with calico-printing mills right up from Croydon down to Wandsworth, near Putney.   In 1805, there were as many as twelve calico printing factories in that region employing about 3,000 men.   The running water of the Wandle was utilized for the driving of the mills.   Calicoes printed in these factories were known by the curious name of " Londrindiana "—evidently showing the Indian origin of the calicoes printed there.

The chief families engaged in the industry were the Ormerods, the Selbies, the Marlars and the Burroughs.   The parish register of Surrey Churches contain numerous entries of calico printers who were apparently men of ample means.   William Ormerod was buried at Mitcham in 1746 (January 29), and he is called a calico printer in the entry.   A will of 1748 mentions one Thomas Marlar, calico printer.   The Mitcham registers also mention Hall, Isaac, son of William, Merrick—all calico-printers.   In an entry of 1719, one William Taylor is called a calico-printer, but in 1722 the same is called a Whitster in another entry.   This is significant in view of the rigorous application of the statute of 1720 which penalized calico printing.

Even after Lancashire became prominent in the cotton industry, Surrey still kept up its calico-printing without any of the mechanical devices that made Lancashire ultimately supreme. At least in the eighteenth century, the Wandle banks printed more calicoes than Lancashire, and it was a prominent industrial centre of the time.   But early in the nineteenth century Lancashire made rapid strides and ruled out all rivals, both at home and abroad.

(For a fuller account, see the Author's paper in the *English Historical Review*, April, 1924.)

INDEX

INDEX

For Product Safety Concerns and Information please contact our EU
representative GPSR@taylorandfrancis.com
Taylor & Francis Verlag GmbH, Kaufingerstraße 24, 80331 München, Germany

www.ingramcontent.com/pod-product-compliance
Ingram Content Group UK Ltd.
Pitfield, Milton Keynes, MK11 3LW, UK
UKHW020929280425
457818UK00025B/61